Learning Re-Enabled

by Susan Orloff OTR/L

Notes

Learning Re-Enabled

by Susan Orloff OTR/L

Published by Children's Special Services, LLC.

Atlanta, Georgia

Printed in the United States of America

ISBN No 0-9716005-0-3

Dedication:

In loving memory of my parents, Lillian Levinson Schriber,

and Max Schriber, your lessons in life and love live on as

a vibrant guide and a loving benediction.

Ambrose Bierce

US. Political Journalist

1842-1914(?)

Road, n.

A strip of land along which one may pass from

where it is too tiresome to be to where

it is futile to go.

And so this pessimistic view of life in the early part of the last century seems very close to what some children are probably feeling about their daily life in school.

It is anxiety-provoking and tiresome to go to a place everyday where, no matter how hard you may try—*you fail*.

TABLE OF CONTENTS

Introduction

This book is all about you, the Listener, the Hearer, the Sayer. Whether you are a teacher or a therapist or a parent, this is about COMMUNICATION.

How to say it.

How to ask it.

How to hear it.

There is no way to delete emotion. The information is hard to say, hard to hear and hard to decipher.

To the parent:

This is **Your Kid**. No one knows them better.

To the teacher:

You know them thoroughly in task and socially specific situations.

To the therapist:

This is the child you have looked at through the microscope of acumen; you've got their style nailed.

How can all these essential people coalesce pro-actively? How can they become cooperating citizens of this child's Babel when they all speak a different language from the heart? How in the world to reach accurate interpretations of all our crucial messages?

So this book is about your needs, given by a former special education teacher, a parent of learning-disabled children and a practicing occupational therapist.

Children's Special Services, LLC.
Mission Statement

It is the mission of Children's Special Services, LLC., to provide quality care to both parents and children. This is not a job for us. It is a calling. It is a privilege to contribute to the developmental process of your child. We consider it our responsibility to help assure that the children in our care acquire the social, emotional, and physical skills necessary for successful growth and maturity. We believe in potential. We strive to motivate. We understand that change is never easy and that growth is sometimes painful. Our goal is to help facilitate the self-structuring of personal goals. We understand the grief of missing the goal. We know that parents hurt as much as the children do, and sometimes more. It is our mission to help children confront and conquer their fears and find joy in the process of becoming. We recognize that change comes from within, it cannot be imposed upon anyone. Every family is sovereign. Every child precious. We honor the trust you have placed in us.

How to use this book, and what it can do (and not do) for you.

This book is designed to help decipher the maze of information and the confusing, often pressured decisions that parents and teachers (as well as individuals themselves) feel when confronted with situations implying a learning disability.

This book is designed to answer the *what*...is a learning disability; ...*what* is "normal development"...*when* should extended help be pursued...*how* to go about getting help...and *how* to help your child at home.

It does not answer why you, why your child, or why did this happen. For that, there are no answers. Of the billions of cells that combine and re-combine as an individual is being formed before, at and after birth, many of those combinations are a result of chance random pairings as well as those predetermined by genetics. This is no one's fault.

This book is not designed to help you diagnose your child; for that, you need specialized testing from an educational and developmental psychologist.

The first part of this book describes what a learning disability is and is not. It illustrates how we learn and how we can adapt learning styles for success. The next part scopes out developmental frameworks, what the "average" (whatever that means) individual is doing at a particular milestone, and what red flags to respond to or ignore. The last section is a to-do suggestion box, complete with bibliographies, where to buy learning-toys and equipment, and suggested activities.

Remember, that there is no expert you can talk to who will know more about your child than you do. The psychologist, the occupational therapist, the teacher, only sees your child in short capsules of time in very specific situations. You, ultimately, are the one in charge. I have found over the years that the only mistake parents make (me included) is thinking the issues will "grow away;" the nagging feeling you have when your child is three or four can be quieted briefly, but it cannot disappear. Early intervention can help quell the anxiety for both you and your child.

I have written this book to be a conversation between us; parent to parent. I have been where you are, I have walked the walk, and I have talked the talk. I have been spoken to and told flat out, "something is wrong with your child." I have had to find solutions. My children have all gone to college, and are leading independent successful lives. This book is to support you on this uncharted journey towards your personal solutions. Take a deep breath, you are not alone.

Acknowledgements:

Children's Special Services, LLC., exists because of the guidance and generosity of Chris Bonsonatta Doane, MS OTR/L, President of Advanced Rehabilitation Services. She let me participate in the development of her company, Advanced Rehabilitation Services, which specializes in staffing and continuing education.

Originally, Children's Special Services was a division of Advanced Rehabilitation Services. Upon Chris's insistence, we made Children's Special Services, LLC., a separate entity. Chris, this book is a tribute to your support and confidence in me. Your wisdom and friendship continues to guide me, nurture me, and sustain me.

Children's Special Services, LLC., would not be possible without the support staff from Advanced Rehabilitation Services, Inc.; so to Teddi, Bobbi, Beth and Lorraine, *Thank You* for always being there for me. You all are consistently supporting me, handling workshops and assisting with staffing. To former ARS therapist, Pam Dillard, I wish to say a most sincere *Thank You*, for your patience with me as I learned how to run a business, pace clients, and mentor additional therapists. It has been a pleasure to be part of your professional and personal life.

To all the children with whom I have worked over the years, thank you for briefly letting me into your lives. A special *Thank You* to all the children who came in on a sunny summer weekend morning so that the photos you see in this book could be taken, a very special *Thank You* to Allison & Austin LaBreque, Kaitlin Mullen, Eric Campos, Andy Howell and Phillip & Nathan Brown.

Thank You also to the many professionals and school principles and directors who had faith in me and allowed occupational therapy into their curriculums when even the words seemed weird and out-of-place. To the faculties and staff at the Heiskell School, Greenfield Hebrew Academy, The Schenk School, Woodward Academy, Mt. Vernon Presbyterian School, Eaton Learning Labs, Dunwoody Prep Pre-School, Kehelliat Chaim Pre-School, Infants of Dunwoody, and the Epstein School, and the Davis Academy all in the Atlanta, Georgia area. *Thank You* for helping me make my professional dreams come true.

This book would never have come to be without the guidance, corrections, interjections, creativity, enthusiasm, direction, and support of Patricia DiBona, my editor, book designer, and friend extraordinaire. Kelly Teasley, whose sensitive and intuitive paintings are included both on the cover and throughout the book are inspirational.

And last but not least, to my children, Jenny, Rachel and Nathan. Seeing their learning struggles through their eyes has allowed me to help other children with more clarity.

And to David, my husband and best friend, all of this is possible because you constantly support and sustain me.

Notes

If you have

ever felt . . .

Why me?

Why my child?

How can this be?

Where do I go?

What does this mean?

Why, didn't my pediatrician

/doctor pick this up?

Where do I start?

Can this be fixed?

Why OT?
And what can it do and not do for my needs.

The possibility exists that if you have inquired about our services, you are either a parent or a teacher, a therapist, or an individual with a learning disability.

It is the mission of this book to talk with and to you. Irrespective of what you may feel inside, what kids on the playground have said, or a boss made you feel, YOU are not "damaged goods." We all have our unique style of doing things. If we were all the same we would all be "Einsteins," Olympic sports stars, and world-renowned scientists. *Where to go, what to do, how to do it, what to expect*: It is the intent of our services to answer these key questions and to give you a foundation from which to be both an informed consumer, and an advocate for yourself, your child or your student.

Your reactions are normal, and they need to be addressed, acknowledged, and responded to with empathy and constructive support.

So, if you have ever felt:

Why me? Why my child? How can this be! Where do I go? What does this mean? Why didn't my pediatrician/doctor pick this up? Where do I start? Can this be fixed? Those are often the first set of questions parents/children and other "first time hearers" ask themselves and anyone they feel they can trust, or in whom they have placed educational confidence. The denial, the anger, the need to control, if taken at face value are obnoxious, distancing behaviors that impede rather than impel parents into pro-active positive directions and, ultimately, solutions for their child's learning issues.

They are good questions. They are valid. However, they are more than that. They are lifelines, not yet attached, not yet secured, which if allowed to tether properly, will serve to guide both the parent and the child into safer waters.

The parents must simultaneously learn the lingo, make discriminating choices, and trust at a time when literally they feel as if they were transplanted onto proverbial shifting sands.

And then some matter-of-fact administrator, or teacher, or psychologist plays "Sargent Friday" and just 'gives 'em the facts,' and we well intentioned professionals wonder in amazement just why these supposedly well educated people are so "weird!!"

It is from this vantage point that parents read the initial reports; in unfamiliar lingo, while sitting on unfamiliar shifting sands. Often on those reports the recommendation is to have an "occupational therapy" evaluation. More new words, more new people, more trusting what is foreign, more fear. Parents come into occupational therapy not knowing what to expect, protective of their child, half-hearing, whole heart hoping this will "fix it."

Thus comes the second set of questions: How much? How long?, How often? It is a time of emotional free-fall for parent and child, and the job of guiding that flight often falls to the pediatric occupational therapist.

Children's Special Services, LLC., in conjunction with Advanced Rehabilitation Services, was founded upon the indefatigable belief that it is to the family that therapy is being provided, not just the child. One or two hours a week will be seven times more effective if techniques are supported in the home. We are a team and we can only win, if everyone contributes to the game.

The careful application of sensory integrative, cognitive, perceptual, and developmental therapies is the essence of individualized occupational therapy. The stuff parents and teachers see, coloring, cutting, drawing, building, playing, remembering, happen only after the attainment of specific neuro-sensory developmental abilities have reached a level of meaningful processing. Ferreting out the difference between a resistive behavior, and a child whose perceptual system is unstable, is the art of occupational therapy. Understanding the neural muscular organic systems influencing these reactions is the science of occupational therapy. The therapeutic application of activity is the culmination of both the art (intuitive) and the science (factual) of play and class simulation in occupational therapy.

However, with the art and science must come the empathy. Both parent and child are entering a situation fraught with uncertainties. It is the job of the occupational therapist to calm the fears and make familiar that which is not.

No pediatric occupational therapy program can be successful without the comments and participation of the parents. They are the foundation from which we begin our work together. We all exist within the context in which we live; our homes, our families, our friends, our jobs. For children, their "job" is going to school. It is what they must do, everyday. For some children, just the act of entering the classroom can be overwhelming.

To manage fears, find solutions, expand choices, discover inner trust—These are the real goals of occupational therapy. When that happens, all the rest of the fabulous puzzle called your child comes together.

Susan N. Schriber Orloff, OTR/L is the Executive Director and CEO of Children's Special Services, LLC., She has been an occupational therapist for over 30 years, and has worked in schools, hospitals, clinics, and home-based pediatric situations. Children's Special Services, LLC., is affiliated with Advanced Rehabilitation Services, Inc., a community leader in advocacy for patients, families, and professional quality assurance.

Notes

SECTION ONE
Learning Disability
in Plain English

Kids Who are Different

Here's to the kids who are different.

The kids who don't always get A's.

The kids who have ears twice

The size of their peers,

And noses that go on for days...

Here's to the kids who are different.

The kids they call crazy or dumb.

The kids who don't fit,

With the guts and the grit,

Who dance to a different drum...

Here's to the kids who are different.

The kids with the mischievous

streak.

For when they have grown,

As history's shown,

It's their difference that

Makes them unique.

Digby Wolfe

What is a learning *difference*?
What is a learning *disability*?

".Mr. and Mrs. Smith, John seems to have some developmental issues."

"I don't want my kid labeled!—It might wind up in writing!"

And so the *dance* begins—an off beat dance, with syncopated rhythms, in both major and minor chords.

Definitions in Plain English:

Learning differences:
A child whose style for learning is negatively deviant from the "norm," and appears to be hampering the initiation, completion, or retention of needed materials.

Learning disability:
A person with one or two specific areas of difficulty, while everything else tests well within average or, in many cases, above average to superior ranges.

IQ:
A specific measure of intelligence that is a composite of verbal and performance scores. Verbal scores are non-motor, where performance scores are cognitive motor.

Attention Deficit Disorder:
A description of behaviors that describe difficulty attending, retaining, organizing, and producing specific tasks. This can be accompanied, but not always, by hyperactivity; which in addition to the above-mentioned behaviors is complicated by random and, at times, uncontrolled motor responses.

Grapho-motor:
Skills inclusive of planning and execution; with and without visual stimuli.

Handedness:
The development of a dominant hand for writing and manipulation.

Muscle tone vs strength:
Muscle tone is the ability to sustain co-contraction in both dynamic and static modes; strength is force exerted on an object *(the ability to use more than one muscle group to maintain a position).*

Visual motor:
The ability to visually organize and associate visual stimuli.

Midline development:
Skills that allow for focal manipulation at the center of the body with peripheral flow from the right to the left.

Peripheral vs. focal vision:
Normally 80% of the average persons vision is peripheral; 20% is focal. Children with visual perceptual issues usually have these percentages reversed.

Vestibular disorder:
Responsible for left/right coordination, eye movements, balance, and tactile interpretations. It is located in the semicircular canals and labyrinths of the ear. Interference here can contribute to eschewed sensory processing, which in turn can contribute to both behavioral and learning issues.

Some Common *Classroom* Signs of Discrete LD.

1. inattentive

2. disorganized

3. needs repeated instructions

4. easily frustrated

5. takes long time to do work

6. poor handwriting

7. social issues (mild to moderate)

8. seems very bright, but just not "getting it done"

Some Common *Home* Signs of Discrete LD.

1. problems with dressing and self-cares beyond anticipated age of competency

2. looses personal items

3. forgets familiar chores/homework

4. difficulty with co-operative tasks

5. difficulty with personal space

6. overly sensitive with family members and friends

7. rejects or demonstrates an unusual amount of fear in slightly familiar or unfamiliar situations

8. not many or new friends

DEFINITIONS OF OCCUPATIONAL THERAPY

School-Based Occupational Therapy

Occupational therapy is a related support service that is initiated as an intervention after other traditional educational methods have been tried. It must be based on educational goals, and support objectives as written in the student's IEP.

Therapy duration and session length is decided by the IEP team (teacher, county representative, therapist, psychologist, school support services personnel and parent).

Services can either be direct or indirect. Direct therapy direct services (fine motor, perceptual motor, sensory training, ADL's, technological modifications, etc.) are usually small group or one-on-one with the student or in inclusion class settings. Sometimes these services are directly delivered by a COTA under the supervision of an OTR.

Indirect services are usually consultative. The OTR consults with other educational staff (classroom teacher, resource teacher, educational specialists, etc.) as to the special issues, needs and concerns and provides suggestions for adaptations and or modifications as needed. In this situation the therapist may also meet with the student on a limited basis.

Private Occupational Therapy

Not restricted by the limits of an individual education plan (IEP); private occupational therapy can integrate all aspects of development: sensory, motor, visual, emotional. Therapy duration and session length is determined collaboratively by both the parent and the therapist.

How OT Helps Learning

0-18 Months	**19-36 Months**
Reflex Reactions	Sensory Awareness
Infant Protective Responses	Tactile
Survival Mechanism	Temperature
	Sound
1	Smell 2
36 Months-5 Years	**Functional End Products**
Neuro/Sensory Organization	Drawing
Balance	Coloring
Perception	Writing
Visual Discrimination	Numbers
Fine Motor Manipulation	Graphs
Gross Motor Planning	Reading
	Copying
3	etc. 4

Notes

Occupational Therapy

addresses boxes

1, 2, and 3,

so that the "stuff"

of school, box 4,

becomes much easier.

N o t e s

What is Sensory Integration?

Sensory integration is the ability of the brain to receive, interpret and act upon accurate incoming information to produce desired cognitive motor responses.

Don't be put off by the lingo—

This is what we all do

everyday without

thinking about it.

The elements of sensory integration are:

Proprioception:
Muscle-bone-joint awareness; the ability to know what position your body is in without vision.

Kinesthesia:
An internal map that lets you know which way to go and how to move.

Diadokokensia:
Communication across the two hemispheres of the brain that are primary for right/left coordination.

Body position in space:
The ability to know "which end is up."

Tactile perception:
The ability to know if you are being touched, and to discriminate what you are touching; as well as pressure and intensity.

Localization of tactile stimuli:
The ability to know where you are being touched.

Vestibular responses:
Inner ear balance mechanisms that also coordinate the eyes and allow for crossing the midline.

Auditory perception:
The ability to discriminate sounds.

Localization of auditory stimuli:
The ability to tell where sounds are coming from.

Auditory defensiveness:
A noxious response to sound.

Auditory confusion:
An inability to discriminate and isolate sounds when in the presence of distracting background noises.

Gross Motor vs. Fine Motor

Gross motor:
Large muscle movements that primarily contribute to mobility and stability patterns as well as ambulation and gross postural adjustments.

Fine motor:
Small muscle movements that control dexterity inclusive of the refined movements of the hands, tongue, eyes, toes, as well as discrete postural adjustments.

Some Frequently Asked Questions:
"My kid is the star soccer player, how can he have motor problems?"

The answer: Soccer is a gross motor activity that requires, on the elementary levels, minimal to moderate precision. In addition, because it is a large motor, constant movement activity, children with some signs of attention issues find this "constant go" sport in agreement with their inner moment.

"Why didn't my doctor or the preschool teacher note this?"
The answer: Physicians are trained to look for systemic and developmental milestone attainment. If the child is well physically, and is walking, running, etc. within normal limits, they may appear "fine." Doctors are not trained to look at the "style" in which a child is accomplishing specific tasks; which is often one of the primary indicators of motor issues.

"Why didn't the pre-school teacher alert me?"
The answer: Children attend pre-school earlier and earlier in their young lives. Day care situations are concerned with the well being of your child and if they are "happy." Pre-first and kindergarten teachers often see that a child is performing differently from others, but may be hesitant to approach the parent for several reasons. Some of the most common reasons are: 1) They are not diagnosticians. 2) They have (probably) not done any formal testing. 3) Often parents become defensive. This is not news they understand or want to hear. They often prefer to believe the child will "outgrow" the problem.

Put your questions here. If they are not answered seek out a professional that you trust to get those issues addressed.

Occupational Therapy

helps by giving the child

the internal abilities to

receive, organize and utilize

required information.

"What is the academic relevance?"

The answer: The academic situation requires that one be able to fixate, organize, integrate, and feedback specific information in a sequential logical order. If a child is having difficulty staying in a chair, is poorly organized, cannot cross the midline of his body and has muscle tone that sends inappropriate signals (to hold the pencil too tight or too loose for example), then performing even the most simple of classroom tasks can become overwhelming. An overwhelmed child becomes a defeated child, and a defeated child fails, even those with superior intelligence.

"How is occupational therapy compatible and of assistance to classroom situations, tutoring, speech, etc.? Why won't just tutoring help?"

The answer: Tutoring is one-on-one education; that is more of the same only individualized. It does not fix neuromuscular issues. Speech, which has its foundation in the neuromotor arena, is a small muscle skill. Often it is important to get the larger muscles to do first what you want the smaller ones to eventually attain.

Occupational therapy helps in the classroom by giving the child the internal abilities to receive, organize and utilize required information. *Occupational therapy* works on these internal abilities. If the child is not constantly moving, is able to write and read what is written, finish work on time, then success in the classroom is enhanced.

Tutoring is important because it reinforces hard-to-grasp concepts and procedures in a private safe environment.

The classroom is important because, in addition to facts, the child learns invaluable social skills.

Speech is important because, in addition to articulation, it teaches receptive and expressive language skills.

Occupational therapy is important because it teaches the underlying skills, and the neuromotor organizational abilities which are at the foundation of all learning.

What is Visual Perception?

Visual perception is the brain's ability to receive, interpret, and act upon visual stimuli. Perception is based on the following seven elements:

Read first, and then list what issues you notice in your child?

1. visual discrimination

The ability to discern one shape from another.

2. visual memory

The ability to remember a specific form when removed from your visual field.

3. visual-spatial relationships

The ability to recognize forms that are the same, but may be in a different spatial orientation.

4. visual form constancy

The ability to differentiate similar forms that may be different in size, color, or spatial orientation, and to consistently match the similar forms.

5. visual sequential memory

The ability to recall 2 to 7 items in sequence with vision occluded.

6. visual figure ground

The ability to discriminate discrete forms when camouflaged or partially hidden.

7. visual closure

The ability to recognize familiar forms that are only partially completed.

©CSS, LLC 2000

For the most part

you can find

samples of these

on the internet:

AOTA.ORG

The evaluations

described here, like many

other generalizations,

are unique to children's

special services. When

seeking an occupational

therapy evaluation ask

beforehand what tools

they use.

Scope of Occupational Therapy

Occupational therapy is a treatment that is medically based to provide both habilitation and rehabilitation to individuals experiencing difficulties in daily life functions. With children, this includes—but is not limited to—assistance with the attainment of age appropriate motor and visual perceptual abilities.

What is a CSS,LLC Occupational Therapy Evaluation?

An occupational therapy program is designed after a complete evaluation. Many tools are used for the evaluation. Some are standardized; meaning it is scored on a statistical standard, some are criterion referenced; meaning performances are judged on an average performance scale for a specific age group. Another form is clinical observation; the OTR's look at the style & form with which the child does specific tasks.

An explanation of some of the evaluative tools is given below.

Explanation of Standardized Tests

The ETCH

is a standardized test of handwriting performance; evaluating legibility size, formation, writing line awareness, spacing and sequencing. A score of 95% is considered fluid writing. Inclusive in the test samples are near- and far-point copy skills as well as dictation and number writing.

The functional neuro-assessment

tests how the child approaches, executes and completes specific developmental tasks. The functional assessment of neuromotor abilities tests the child's functional responses in play/game situations. It factors visual, sensory, motor and cognitive components of task.

The Goodenough-Harris Drawing Test

is a test of fine motor-cognitive/organizational abilities as well as body image.

The PEER

is a multi-task evaluation that combines neuro-developmental, behavioral and health components. It provides normative scored observations that help define developmental areas of concern. It evaluates developmental attainment, associated observation, neuro-maturation, as well as a task-analysis of the input (visual, verbal, sequential, somesthetic), storage (short-term memory, experiential acquisition) and output (fine motor, motor sequence, verbal sequence and verbal expressive) functions.

The Visual Motor Inventory (VMI)

and the sub-tests for visual perception and motor abilities is a standardized test that evaluates both the visuo-motor, and the visual *and* motor abilities in isolation. This test is used to help identify significant difficulties in the areas of co-ordination and perceptual motor and non-motor integration.

The Wide Range Assessment of Visual Motor Abilities

tests the child in the three spheres of visual motor/perceptual development. It provides a psychometrically sound assessment of visual-motor, visual spatial, and fine motor skills. A score of 50 % with a standard score of 100 is considered within the average range.

The Test of Visual-Perceptual Skills (non-motor)

tests all of the same areas as the VMI, with the elimination of the motor component. Thus it is able to ferret out that which is perception vs. motor. It is these discrete visual perceptual abilities that are essential for comprehensive and organized, receptive and expressive, motor production.

The Handwriting Without Tears Evaluation

Is a criterion referenced test of paper/pencil production that looks at habituated responses from memory and with a sample.

The Sensory modulation/regulation assessment

looks at the sensory systems of tactile, visual, proprioceptive, vestibular, auditory, taste/oral, and olfactory observing both attentional and regulatory responses.

The OT "Play/Sensory" Evaluation

looks at task approach, language, and behavior in various novel motor tasks.

Sensory History is a standardized checklist formulated by Winnie Dunn, OTR for the purpose of determining which situations elicit overly alert behavioral responses. It covers auditory, visual, tactile, movement, body position, emotional/social, and activity level responses. It is scored as *Always*, *Frequently*, *Occasionally*, *Seldom* and *Never*.

Ask how long the evaluation takes.

Because it individuates to each clinic and the therapist(s). Ask about time, cost and if you can observe before the test date.

Ask how long the course of therapy will take.

Again, dependent upon the issues found. At Children's Special Services, LLC., the usual length of therapy is one school-year *and* a summer to insure carry-over. Treatment is usually once a week for 50 minutes. Depending upon the school, many private schools allow Children's Special Services, LLC., to come into the school and provide services on site. Ask your therapist and school about this.

The Essence of Occupational Therapy

Occupational therapy addresses all of the above to reconstruct the neural motor, psychosocial foundations of development and learning so that the functional results will be commensurate with the desired outcomes, producing both an intellectual and emotionally gratifying experience.

How does your child express this?

What an Occupational Therapy Evaluation looks at:

Behaviors

ATNR

Asymetrical tonic

neck reflex

> **VISION:**
> Tracking
> Convergence
> Quick localization

STNR

Symetrical tonic

neck reflex

> **REACHING PATTERNS:**
> **GRASP RELEASE PATTERNS:**
> Bimanual functions
>   cutting
>   reaching for a ball (w/ w/o 2 hands)
> Rapid forearm rotations (diadokokinesia)
> Isolated finger control
> Strength and range of motion
> Muscle tone
> Equilibrium
> UE stability/weight shift

These are

stability patterns

necessary for all

flow and go

movements

> **REFLEXES:**
> Protective reactions
> ATNR—STNR
> Schilders arm extension
>   choreathetosis
>   arm position changes
>   discomfort
> Body image
> Handedness
>   copy skills: from board/desk
> Sensory
>   vestibular
>   tactile
>   auditory
> Activities of Daily Living
>   dressing/feeding/toileting

PATHWAYS IN THE BRAIN

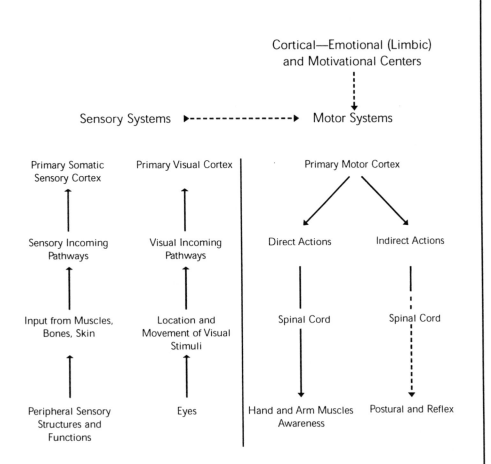

Cortical—Emotional (Limbic)
and Motivational Centers

Sensory Systems ▶------------▶ Motor Systems

Primary Somatic
Sensory Cortex

Primary Visual Cortex

Primary Motor Cortex

Sensory Incoming
Pathways

Visual Incoming
Pathways

Direct Actions

Indirect Actions

Input from Muscles,
Bones, Skin

Location and
Movement of Visual
Stimuli

Spinal Cord

Spinal Cord

Peripheral Sensory
Structures and
Functions

Eyes

Hand and Arm Muscles
Awareness

Postural and Reflex

Physical activity involves the coordination of the sensory motor and limbic (motivational) systems in the brain. The direct motor pathways make for fast movements, the indirect for slower, more modulated, regulated actions, connected within the nervous system to other associated pathways. Adapted from *Essentials of Neural Science and Behavior.*

What is Memory?

Notes

How does your

child respond to

"old" data and

"new" data?

What about

sequences?

What is a Memory?

It is the coordination of the senses imprinting on the brain specific sights sounds, smells, touch and emotional feelings.

It is essential for learning.

There are Three Types of Memory

1. Immediate

Lasts less than one minute.

It contains exact imagery.

For retention must be transferred to:

2. Short-Term memory

Lasts up to a few hours to a week. Functional brain structures involve the hippocampus which is the "organizer" of information before it is transferred to:

3. Long-Term memory

Organization and repetition help to store this information in the cerebral cortex: it is only the basics of the information, many details are obscured.

How Do We Remember?

TOUCH:

Primary sensory input triggers initial memory and
excites something called the Somatosensory Cortex.

SOUND:

Stored on contact in the Primary Auditory Cortex
within the temporal lobe.

SIGHT:

Encoding of the imagery is translated into the nerve
impulses and sent to the Primary Visual Cortex.

TASTE AND SMELL:

Receptors in the nose embellish the previously encoded
memories to produce an enhanced memory "picture."
These are stored in the Olfactory Cortex.

SO..........

IF WE HOPE TO REMEMBER WHAT WE ARE TAUGHT
WE MUST STIMULATE THE SENSES TO LEARN.

Notes

What is your

major concern

specific to home?

Specific to school

Specific to social

situations?

Behaviors Students May Have Who Experience Memory Difficulties

1) Poor organization.

2) Habitually tardy to turn in assignments.

3) Loses books, reports, etc.

4) Anxious.

5) Overwhelms easily.

6) Freezes up.

7) Sloppy.

8) Incomplete assignments/ too brief

9) Works without signs of personal investment.

10) Doesn't follow instructions.

11) Overdependence on aid.

12) Very easily distracted.

This Causes the Teachers to Assume that the Student is:

1) Lazy

2) Arrogant

3) Disrespectful

4) Uncaring

5) Not Working To Potential

6) Inattentive

7) Excuse-Prone

8) Rule-Breaker/Rule-Tester

9) Uncooperative

10) Just needs to try harder

Negative halos

What frustrates you

when you interact with

your child?

What frustrates

you child?

"Negative halos."

What frustrates you

when you interact

with your child?

What frustrates

your child?

What Students with Memory Difficulties are Probably Feeling

1) Inadequate

2) Awkward

3) Unpopular

4) Defensive

5) Alone

6) Confused

7) Like "everyone" is always staring at them

8) Angry

9) Depressed

10) Feeling unsafe-emotionally and physically

What Does the Research Say?

Learning is a melding of both Art and Science. Research in neurobiology confirms that the use of the hands changes the learning process from passive to active, which in turn increases long term memory, especially that of sequences, and stimulates spontaneous creativity.

Life *is* movement, life *is* dynamic, life *is* a dance for both parents and teachers to learn to dance with these children. So remember that chldren who experience memory difficulties usually have deficits
with immediate and short term memory and in addition these children often have above average to superior long term memory and in many cases above average to superior intelligence.

WOW.

If we see it,

we recognize it.

If we touch it,

we know it.

If we move it,

it's ours.

How We Learn

How We Learn

How We Learn

Emotional Intelligence

"is the ability to delay

gratification, maintain

emotional self-control

and be optimistic."

David Hamburg

psychiatrist, President of the
Carnegie Corporation

In a report from the National Center for Clinical Infant Programs,
a child's readiness for school is directly dependent upon the ability and
knowledge of how to learn. How we learn is based upon seven functions:

1) Confidence—a sense of control.

2) Curiosity.

3) Intentionality—the wish to be effective and to
        affect change.

4) Self Control.

5) Relatedness—to be understood by as well as
        understanding others.

6) Communication.

7) Cooperativeness.

Emotional Intelligence

Daniel Goleman describes emotional intelligence as involving the following concepts:

1) Knowing one's emotions—self awareness

2) Managing emotions— handling feelings, building on
   self-awareness

3) Motivating oneself—using emotions for self-motivation,
   mastery, creativity, delaying gratification to reach a goal.

4) Recognizing emotions in others—empathy.

5) Handling relationshops.

Optimum

performance and learning

happens in a

state of flow.

Susan Orloff
OTR

Dealing with Emotions

John Mayer, a psychologist from the University of New Hampshire, states that there are three specific ways in which people deal with emotions:

1) Self aware—

   Aware of moods as they are having them.

2) Engulfed—

   Swamped by emotions, moods are in charge, not the
   person.

3) Accepting—

   Resigned to despair or blindly positive; both groups
   have no motivation to change.

Emotions can overwhelm concentration, that which is being overwhelmed is the cognitive ability psychologists often refer to as *working memory*. Working memory occurs in the *pre-frontal cortex*, where feelings and emotions combine.

Anxiety sabotages intellect, inhibits learning and reduces the quality of judgmental functions.

Good moods enhance flexibility, relaxation, broaden response patterns and increase problem solving abilities.

The ability to contain and reframe emotions is called the "master aptitude."

These children lack the ability to find the "middle ground." They cannot modulate their physical or emotional selves. An intact modulatory system is at the foundation of being able to store and process information. Modulation gives rise to functional support capacities which gives rise to competence with functional end products.

Learning is really about sensory processing. Emotional components are very important. Peer interactions and social style are a strong indicator of possible issues.

Neurologically the emotional center of the brain matures in the following order:

Sensory—Early Childhood

Limbic System—Puberty

Frontal Lobes—Late adolescence to 18 years

The frontal lobes combine the input from the sensory and limbic systems. It is the point of origin of emotional self-control, understanding and planned responses.

Piaget's Theories
Simplified

An Overview of Piaget's Developmental Framework

Piaget's theory believes that specific age-appropriate learning and behaviors happen in a distinct, predictable progression, all within whatever are the child's general developmental circumstances.

He held that learning and growth were a continuous, on-going, lifelong process; and that the *Last Stage*, No. 4, was perpetually open-ended and evolving. And so, what begins in pre-adolescence culminates without finality in the adult.

That *First Stage*, ending at about age 2, is the most complex, with many substages and marked by reflex, visual awareness and the graduation from purely random to evident-stimuli, and from reaction to response.

The *Second Stage*, in those five years between 2 and 7, is shown by the initiation of the ability to copy and accomodate to observed behaviors.

The *Third Stage*, the four years from 7 to 11, is the first intellectual growth spurt; with Language carrying the principal evidence and evolving the child in two categories, communicative and noncommunicative.

Communicative Speech shares thoughts, feelings, ideas and is inclusive of input.from the listener as someone talked-with.
Noncommunicative Speech is a monologue that is often egocentric and repetitive. It is also here, in *Stage 3*, that grander moral judgments build in fresh pictures, but painted by children in intellectual black and white.

And last and longest, *Stage Four*. Where manifold intellectual functions spring to greater and greater life. The classification of things grows, prioritizing of tasks, sequencing, a cinemascopically expanding mental imagery, and the development of **Equilibrium**: the function that allows a person to put things/events/needs in perspective and keep life on an even keel. '*Emotional Intelligence,*' a term of our time, not Piaget's, fits extraordinarily well here. And he would almost certainly have wished he'd thought of it.

> "...Intelligence is the totality of behavior coordinations that characterize behavior at a certain stage"
> **Piaget and Knowledge 245.**

Notes

PIAGET'S FOUR STAGES OF DEVELOPMENT

Stage One: Sensorimotor

Birth to Two years

Random to stimuli reflexive responses

Stage Two: Pre-operational

Two to Seven Years

Symbolic play and increased vocabulary

Stage Three: Concrete Operational

Seven to Eleven Years

Sequential ordering, moral judgements, "fair play"

Stage Four: Formal Stage

Eleven to Adult

Emotional, intellectual, equilibrium

Comparison of Llorens-Ayres-Willbarger and others to Piaget

Piaget's four development divisions interface easily with the works of Ayres, Lorens, Willbarger, Moore and others. The theme of four developmental categories, stages or system processes repeats itself through these many theories and approaches.

Ayres's work with sensory integration, focuses on the development of the child from a sensor-responsive being to one that produces "functional end products" (i.e. competent successful motor-cognitive acts in school and home).

Moore's work with neuro-development answers many of the questions of the how and why specific responses are often illicited with children exhibiting discrete clusters of cognitive-motor performances.

Llorens addresses the areas of sensory input, and follows it through the neural pathways to the (hopefully) desired motor output, thus creating a functional feedback system so a specific act may be not only repeated, but modified and expanded upon to be utilized in more complex situations.

In each case these highly respected developmental researchers have demonstrated a consistency in categorizing their theories into four distinct groupings. This consistency cannot be regarded as coincidental when superimposed upon a basic neurological model, which can also be grouped into four areas: 1) central nervous system, 2) peripheral nervous system, 3) the sympathetic, and 4) the parasympathetic systems.

Utilizing the neurological framework for learning, a set of four developmental skills evolves: 1) motor sensory, 2) cognitive, 3) psychosocial (intrapersonals) and 4) social (interpersonal). These skills are essential for the creation of, as Ayres would phrase it, "functional end products," or as Llorens would term this "functional feedback." Whatever it is termed, these are elements necessary for success, not just in school, but in life.

Developing a criterion referenced assessment that analyzes how a child performs a specific function, in addition to quantitive standardized tests allows the therapist to utilize the assessment process. The statistical and the inferential data forms the foundation for the creation of functionally-based goals and treatment.

Notes

1. FRONTAL LOBE:
Planning
Expressive Speech
Speech
Movement

2. PARIETAL LOBE:
Touch
Taste

3. OCCIPITAL LOBE:
Sight

4. TEMPORAL LOBE:
Receptive Spech

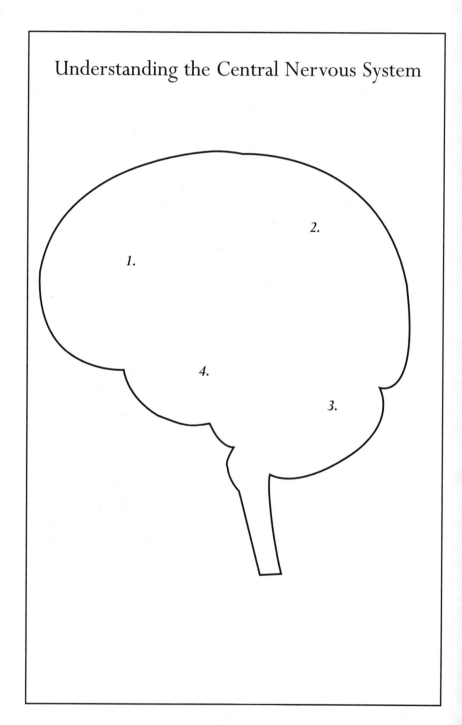

Understanding the Central Nervous System

Structures and Functions of the Central Nervous System

1. CORPUS CALLOSOM

   Information from right to left

2. BASAL GANGLIA

   Controls movement, cognition

3. AMYGDALA

   Heart Beat

   emotions

4. THALMUS

   Relay station to

   the brain

5. HYPOTHALAMUS

   Sex, temperature, blood pressure

6. PITUITARY

   The "Master gland:"

   hormones/growth

7. HIPPOCAMPUS

   Long term memory

8. MID BRAIN

   (Pons, Medulla)

   Breathing, circulation,

   digestion, heartbeat

9. CEREBELLUM

   Coordination of

   movement.

SECTION TWO
Guidelines for Parents

The How, When, Why of Occupational Therapy for Parents of School-aged Children

Your child might need an occupational therapy screening, if you or the teacher suspect that there is a performance gap between them and their peers.

- If your child frustrates easily

- Rejects unfamiliar tasks

- Prefers to play alone rather than with friends

- Seems to have difficulty transitioning from one task to another

- Poor or slow fine-motor skills

- Clumsy

- Seems to be unusually forgetful

- School is a struggle

- Social issues dominate school concerns

- Doesn't want to go to school

- Depressed

- Endurance

Visual motor:

The ability to visually organize and associate visual stimuli.

Midline development:

Skills that allow for focal manipulation at the center of the body with peripheral flow from the right to the left.

Peripheral vs. focal vision:

Normally 80% of the average persons vision is peripheral; 20% is focal. Children with visual perceptual issues usually have these percentages reversed.

Vestibular disorder:

Responsible for left/right coordination, eye movements, balance, and tactile interpretations. It is located in the semicircular canals and labyrinths of the ear. Interference here can contribute to eschewed sensory processing, which in turn can contribute to both behavioral and learning issues.

Some Common *Classroom* Signs of Discrete LD.

1. inattentive

2. disorganized

3. needs repeated instructions

4. easily frustrated

5. takes long time to do work

6. poor handwriting

7. social issues (but not severe)

8. seems very bright, but just not "getting it done"

Some Common *Home* Signs of Discrete LD.

1. problems with dressing and self-cares beyond anticipated age of competency

2. looses personal items

3. forgets familiar chores/homework

4. difficulty with co-operative tasks

5. difficulty with personal space

6. overly sensitive with family members and friends

7. rejects or demonstrates an unusual amount of fear in slightly familiar or unfamiliar situations

8. not many or new friends

Notes

Don't jump

the gun— If in

doubt get a

second opinion from

an objective professional.

What have you

noticed about your

child?

COMPETENCIES NEEDED FOR SCHOOL SUCCESS

Neurological

Hearing

Balance---gravitational responses

Tactile

Visual

Cognitive (inclusive of attentional issues)

Emotional

Peer interactions

Authority responses

Frustration levels

Task initiation/response patterns

Group skills

Physical

Mobility

Self-cares

Hand skills

Strength

Intellectual

Performance

Task Behaviors (rejection, motivation, curiosity, transitional skills, initiation, organization.)

Time Concepts (sequencing, getting work done "on time," etc.)

Task Production (following directions–verbal, written, demonstrated, repeated, etc.)

Retention (long vs. short-term memory issues–ADD children)

Task Judgments (relies on teacher, peers, independent)

Questions Parents Ask:

If my child gets therapy the school will assume there is something wrong with them and equate this with low intelligence.

Getting a bright child help, helps them from becoming discouraged and defeated. It also breaks the academic mind set that if they only "tried harder, they could do it" and the reason they are not is willfulness. A competent therapist will communicate to the class-room teacher just what and why certain techniques are being used so that this can be replicated in the classroom to help ensure increase productivity and success.

What if I get my child help, and they still have problems? Won't I make things worse if I get accommodations and school issues persist?

No! Your child is smart enough to know something is not "quite right." Your child is smart, they already feel "different." With the special service specialist, set realistic expectations for yourself, your child, and the teacher. Ask about what and how long a particular intervention is projected to take. Emphasize to the child that this is not some-thing that is going to be necessarily fast, and that it is not being done to them but with their full cooperation.

How do I answer my friends and family when they say that I am over-reacting? They tell me that I should just let my kid be a "kid," that they are bright and I shouldn't "stir up stuff."

The 'stuff is already stirred. Your child receiving help, HELPS—**period**.
Old stereotypes and clichés die slow and hard. These individuals are speaking through their own fears and misconceptions. They have not sat in the meetings, they have not read the reports, they have not talked to professionals, and they have not seen the daily turmoil your child is in. ***Don't listen!*** This is an informed decision that you as a parent have made after careful considerations and consultations; and in response to your child's expressed (physical, emotional verbal) discomforts.

How do I include the educational setting in the therapy process?

Good communication helps to make the teacher feel like an intrinsic part of the aca-demic team and an enabler for the child's success. Since it is by law the "job" of the school to teach, then helping the teacher teach. If gone with awareness of each par-ticular school's mission it will only enhance the success of all involved—the school, the teacher, the therapist, and most important the child.

Competence is self-perpetuating and helps.....

It is not about bright—

In fact, the reason that

this type of child has

been able to succeed

so far is that they are very

bright and have discovered

ways to accommodate

and facilitate

successful outcomes

Notes

Your child is the

KEY member of

this team!

Nothing happens without them being consistently present emotionally, intellectually, and physically. Sometimes it will be hard. Sometimes they may feel like "nothing is happening."

Acknowledge these very real feelings. They are used to not quite getting "it" right. Emotionally they are prepared to fail, not succeed. An essential part of therapy is to change this "in the rut" thinking.

Your support is essential!! Re-direct their thinking. Make analogies about something they learned (like riding a bike) that was once hard and now easy.

What should I expect from therapy? When will I notice a change?

You should expect therapy to be like any new experience for your child. If they adjust easily to new situations then the start will be more spontaneous than for the child who resists change and/or new situations.

Expect stops and starts as therapy progresses. Your child knows they are being brought somewhere to fix something. Although they may want it "fixed," they may resent having to need any type of intervention.

Support the therapy process by explaining why they are going. Do not make it a discussion. This was a decision you made after careful consideration. Do not bargain. This is not negotiable. For therapy to work, the process is initiated in treatment and supported at home. "OT homework" should be taken as seriously as school homework.

Progress depends on commitment.

Changes will be subtle at first. A child who came to therapy with three shirts on, may reduce the need to be covered, indicating a normalization of his tactile system. Another child who is generally a couch potato may want to go out to play; while another who is clumsy may be demonstrating more agility.

Progress is often met with resistance on the part of the child. This stranger is asking them to give up a way of doing something, however maladaptive, and, on faith, try something new with only the therapist's word that it will be worth the effort to learn and use it. Traditional learning is hard for these children, they have had problems with it, and now this relative stranger is asking them to learn something unfamiliar in an unfamiliar way in an unfamiliar setting. WOW!!! This is very threatening to your child. And when threatened people react with rejection, anger and fear. Your child is no different. That is why your support is vital to the success of therapy.

Why is my child a Wiz on the computer, but can't do work in class? Why not just give him a lap-top to work with instead of paper & pencil?

Computers are useful tools after the child has attained adequate in-hand manipulation skills. These skills can only be acquired by using one's own hands, and putting your forefinger on a mouse, or moving a joystick or an adapted keyboard cannot replace the agility learned through "old fashioned" play: jacks, finger painting, hand looms, lacing crafts, etc. Computers reinforce straight-ahead, focal vision-play and not peripheral vision (surrounding side stimuli). A child who does not develop this at a young age may have difficulty picking up on visual cues in the classroom, i.e., blackboard work, the following of sequences and visual tracking.

Why isn't my child having fun in OT, like he did at the beginning? I want my child to be happy!

There is a difference between happiness and fun. Fun does not add to one's abilities. Happiness is intrinsically related to the attainment of skills and subsequent feelings of competency; which in turn increase one's emotional security. The path to this security is often hard won. Your job, as parent, is to keep them motivated through this unfamiliar and challenging process.

Evaluation Elements

What is the most important behavioral pattern in your family?

How does (or doesn't) your child express this?

If you could only have one thing you could change, what would it be?

Data:

    Date of Evaluation:

    Date of Birth:

    Name:

    Parents Name:

    Address:

    Phone Number:

    Grade:

    Teacher:

Background Information:

    Psychological tests:

    Any special services currently receiving:

    Family background:

    Illnesses:

    Developmental milestones:

Ask for your "Parents' Bill of Rights" (read it; every state school system has one set up)

DON'T GIVE UP— BE PERSISTENT.

Attitude During Tests:

    Withdrawn:

    Attentive:

    Hyperactive:

    Needed repetitions:

    Followed directions:

    Fear of failure:

Tests Administered:

    Standardized:

    Formal observations:

Results:

Summary:

Goals:

N o t e s

Remember—

This is a snap-shot

of your child on a

particular day,

at a particular time.

Try to see these

specific results

in generalities as

well as absolutes.

The following is a sample occupational therapy evluation

Notes

OCCUPATIONAL THERAPY EVALAUTION

Name: Xxxxxxx	DOB: 0-0-00
Parent(s): PPPPPPPPP	Age: 00.0
Address: Anywhere	Grade 00: grader
Phone: 000-000-000(day) 000-000-000(evening)	School: Any School
Eval Date 0-0-00	Referred: by ZZZZZZZZZZZZZZ

Background Information:

Xxxxxxx is the youngest of three children, with her siblings being much older than she is (ages 17 and 20). By report, all developmental milestones were attained within normal limits, and with the exception of ear infections, health history is not remarkable.

In April 2000, Xxxxxxx did have a psychological test administered by Dr.ZZZZZ, at VVVV WWWW Service. The results of this testing were not available at the time of this evaluation. Dr. ZZZZZ referred Xxxxxxx for an occupational therapy evaluation.

Parents report that she is "reluctant to do worksheets" and "doesn't like to write." In addition to the writing issue, they noted both on the intake form and in the discussion after the evaluation, that her task behaviors are a concern. Specifically they note that she has difficulty staying focused, easily distracted, disorganized, and seems to need instructions repeated more than would be expected.

Behaviors During Testing:

Xxxxxxx initially entered the OT clinic hesitantly, holding her doll, "BBB" close to her. After a brief "warm up" period to the clinic, she seemed ready to participate in the assessment procedures.

Throughout the testing, she was observed to need both repeated verbal and demonstrated directions and much reinforcement. There appeared to be a significant fear of failure, and a hesitancy to engage in unfamiliar tasks. In new situations, there seemed to be an increase in both her activity level, and a decrease in the quality of her responses. For example, she would often use "distracters" when presented specific directions , (" draw only a person head-to-toe,") she added "I'll first draw a street." She responded well to redirection, but task procedures needed to be repeated using a tri-sensory (auditory, visual, motor) and structured approach.

Tests Administered

Wide Range Assessment of visual Motor Abilities (WRAVMA)
Test of Visual-Perceptual Skills (non-motor) (TVPS)
Goodenough-Harris Drawing Test
ETCH-evaluation of children's handwriting
Functional assessment of neuro-motor abilities

Results

The Wide Range Assessment of Visual Motor Abilities
tests the child in the three spheres of visual motor/perceptual development. It provides
a psychometrically sound assessment of visual-motor, visual spatial, and fine motor skills.
A score of 50 % with a standard score of 100 is considered within the average range.

Xxxxxxx's scores were as follows:

Test	Raw score	Standard score	Percentile	Age equiv.
Drawing Visual-motor	7	72	3	4.10
Matching Visual-spatial	24	89	23	6.3
Pegboard Fine-motor	29	101	53	7.4*

*On this section, in particular, she often "adapted" responses and had to re-start the task, because her changes were not in keeping with the desired action. For example, she wanted to put "order" to the fine motor manipulative test by first only selecting one color and then trying to make a pattern. The instruction was just to fill the pegboard quickly.

This section assesses in-hand manipulation, speed, and accuracy of placement, crossing the body midline, sustaining a repetitive 2-step task pattern and upper extremity stability/mobility patterns. The specific direction is , "Hold the pegboard with one hand—non-dominant—and place the pegs with your other hand, keeping your "helper" hand on the pegboard so it will not move." Maintenance of these instructions, even after multiple trials, required much repetition and re-direction.

It is felt that this is probably due to a visualization and processing interference at this time. At no time did this therapist assess these responses as defiant or willful. Instead, it was felt that these were her self-initiated adaptive reactions to try to get the task done as close to "right" as possible.

N o t e s

Her desire to please, fear of failure, hesitancy to enter unfamiliar situations and her success and goal-oriented motivators seems to rule out this as "intentional behaviors." Rather it suggests that this is probably a sub-cortical response to help her facilitate visual/perceptual and motor organization.

If this is happening in class, this is probably very frustrating for both Xxxxxxx and her teachers. She seems to understand the direction, but actually does not, so when she goes to implement it, she changes the procedure, which in turn alters the outcome.

On the overall test, she obtained a composite standard score of 82 with a composite percentage of 11%. Throughout this test she had several behaviors that seemed to be negatively impacting the results. She would block out the vision of one eye, with the left hand usually blocking the left eye, but not always sometimes it was right to right, but never across the midline. There was much body "twisting" and maneuvering in her chair, and she often had to be brought back to the tasks. Additionally, she consistently sub-vocalized what she needed to do, but more as a delay than an initiator for the item. She was easily discouraged, often saying, "this is hard"; needing encouragement to try some items. As previously explained, following specific directions was difficult for her.

<u>The Test of Visual-Perceptual Skills</u> (non-motor) tests the seven major visual perceptual arenas, with the elimination of the motor component. Thus, it is able to ferret out that which is perception vs. motor.

Xxxxxxx's scores were as follows:

Test	Raw Score	Perceptual Age	Scaled Score	Percentile Rank
Visual Discrimination	10	7.5	10	50
Visual Memory	9	8.7	11	37
Visual-Spatial				
Relationships	14	12.8	14	91
Visual Form				
Constancy	9	8.1	11	37
Visual				
Sequential				
Memory	10	7.8	11	50

She received a median perceptual age of 9.2 and an average percentile rank of 58%. The sum of her scaled scores equaled 73, which gave a perceptual quotient of 103. The perceptual quotient is statistically linked to projected IQ scores, however it is felt that this score is somewhat lower than might be expected due to the range of her performances.

Visual closure, the ability to see half a form on paper and the other half in your head, is crucial for writing, and this was her lowest performance area.

The Goodenough-Harris Drawing Test:

is a test of fine motor-cognitive/organizational abilities as well as body image. Her raw score was 10, which yielded an age equivalent of 5.2. Although this is slightly higher than the drawing score on the WRAVMA, it is supportive of her issues with visual-motor production. It is important to note that she drew her person with broken arms. In the drawing, the subjects' left arm was in a "cast." Additionally when given the instruction to "draw a person," she said, "first I'll draw a street". The therapist had to turn over the paper and have her start on the other side for her to do the task as directed.

Interpretively, using the House Tree Person Test criteria, the drawing an arm that is broken is often suggestive of feeling in some way "damaged" or "broken." Her desire to first "draw a street" may be another indicator of her need to over stabilize within the visual-perceptual realm. Other testing seems to support that she is mostly likely experiencing perceptual place constancy interference.

The TVPS tests only near-point perception. Difficulty seems to come when she has to look at something from a distance, or visualize it in her head and then produce it on paper.

The ETCH:

is a standardized test of handwriting performance; evaluating legibility size, formation, writing line awareness, spacing and sequencing. A score of 95% is considered fluid writing. She was tested in only the manuscript format.

Her scores were as follows:

Upper case production 73% Lower case production 69.2% Numbers 1-12 66.6
Near point copying 60% Far point copying 60% Dictation numbers 100%*
Dictation letters 33.3%

---

*Although she got all of the numbers in correct order, they were not legible. The 5-9- and 3, were all reversed, and the 8 and 5 were slanted backwards.

Writing was impacted by omissions, sequencing issues, poor line awareness, and size and spacing concerns. Because this therapist was told, in advance that Xxxxxxx did not like to write, this test was given first, to "get it out of the way."

This test supports the previous findings of issues with fine motor ideation to production, referred to as graphomotor abilities.

The functional neuro-assessment:

tests how the child approaches, executes, and completes specific developmental tasks. The functional assessment of neuro-motor abilities tests the child's functional responses in play and life situations. It factors visual, sensory, motor and cognitive components of task, ideation, organization, and execution.

Her results were as follows:

Visual tracking was accomplished with minimal head movement, but was not easily sustained. Convergence was initiated but not completed, holding power was fair and quick localization needed to be accompanied by auditory stimulation.

Reaching patterns: within normal limits.

Grasp and release: completed with a neutral wrist both right and left; crossing the midline with both the right and the left but less frequently with the left. Had difficulty following a 3-step sequential task.

Bimanual functions: with the exception of cutting skills, all were within normal limits.

Diadokokinesia (rapid forearm rotations); irregular and labored in all modes.

Isolated finger control within normal limits.

Range of motion: within normal limits.

Hand strength: within normal limits.

Flexor/extensor control; can assume positions but had difficulty in both prone and supine maintaining them for more than five seconds.

Muscle tone: completed with over stabilization.

Equilibrium: tested in the static mode; completed with fast displacement (again supporting the earlier findings of over stabilization suggesting diminished tone.).

Upper extremity stability/weight shift: unstable, difficulty assuming and/or maintaining the weight on arms/hands position.

Primitive motor reflexes: (these should have been resolved by 18 months of age), all were present.

Functional movement patterns: difficulty ascending and descending stairs, running, hopping and skipping.

Standing balance: impaired both eyes open and closed.

Schilder's arm extension: completed with extreme rigidity, elbows in hyperextension with both trunk rotation and head rotation.

Body image: intact.

Crossing the midline: more on the right than the left.

Dominance: established on the right; when writing she habitually did not hold the paper with her left; holding her head instead. She tends to be perfectionistic, writing was accomplished with an intense 4-finger thumb-wrap grasp.

Copy skills: appeared to loose her place easily, more so with far point copying than near.

Work pace: had to be constantly monitored., she seemed to "freeze" when unsure of a response—"best guessing" was very hard for her.

Sensory responses: stereonosis (identification of familiar object with vision occluded by touch only) within normal limits; position sense grossly intact; proprioception (muscle/bone joint awareness) impaired as was localization of tactile stimuli. Vestibular responses; depressed, there was no nystagmus post first or second rotation.

Dressing skills: dependent –by report.

Summary

Xxxxxxx presents as an initially very shy child who responds well to structure and support. She appeared to be trying her best throughout the testing situation, but seemed to become easily intimidated when situations were unfamiliar.

Following directions, both verbal and demonstrated required sample practice and repetition. She seemed to self-distract herself from the specific task (changing it in an engaging manner) so that she was then following her own agenda. When structured into a specific pattern, a fatigue response was noted.

Visually, Xxxxxxx does not appear to have visual constancy, so that things are constantly shifting within her visual field. It is felt that this is attributing to many of her observed task behaviors. If "things" in her world are constantly "shifting," then to find her "place" she seems to have adopted a rigid and self-directed pattern . 'If I can't follow the exact direction, then I will come as close to it as I can' seems to be her current task style.

This is probably very frustrating for both Xxxxxxx and her teachers; asking her to do specific tasks that always appear to "almost" get done, probably produces dissatisfaction on the part of the teacher, and a feeling of defeat for her.

In the sensory realm, Xxxxxxx also exhibited issues with touch localization, balance, and co-ordination. There appears to be a discontinuity between her accessing a visual "steady state" and the planning of required motor responses both gross and fine.

A program of occupational therapy intervention is suggested to help remediate the above mentioned concerns.

As therapy will begin this summer, suggestions for the classroom teacher will be made closer to the start of school. In addition, it is suggested that at the start of the school year, the direct therapist visit the school to observe the classroom and the meet with both the parents and the teachers to discuss this evaluation and subsequent suggestions.

Children need to move! Limit

computer time!

Xxxxxxx's scores were as follows:

Test Raw score		Standard score	Percentile	Age equiv.
Drawing Visual-motor	7	72	3	4.10
Matching Visual-spatial	24	89	23	6.3
Pegboard	17	81	10	4.4

Goals

1. Normalize tone.
2. Increase ability to follow directions, including sequencing skills.
3. Increase visual perceptual skills.
4. Increase gross motor planning.
5. Increase cutting skills.
6. Increase organizational and sequencing abilities, building to a 3-step non-repetitive pattern.
7. Increase writing abilities starting with the "Calaerobics" worksheets, and then moving later into the cursive Handwriting Without Tears program.

It may be helpful to consider a speech therapy evaluation to assess auditory processing abilities.

It has been a pleasure to evaluate Xxxxxxx. It is suggested that this report be shared with the referring psychologist, teachers, pediatrician, and other related health professionals.

Too much electronics eliminates

the child from being the initiator

of the game.

Susan N. Schriber Orloff, OTR/L
Exec. Director/CEO, Children's Special Services, LLC.
GA. Lic. #870

Toys That Facilitate
Required School Competencies

Toys that have multiple sensory components to which the children are required to respond are best. Many of the toys that are found in therapy catalogues can be found in less expensive versions in places like Target, Wal-Mart, and Toys R' Us; so do not rush to order. Instead use the pictures in the catalogues to find similar toys. They do not have to be exact to be good.

There are no toys that just do one thing. There are toys that do one thing more than the other. However, on the main, common parental/therapeutic/academic sense prevails best.

Neurological competency can be stimulated by toys that encourage and or require touch, movement, sound responsiveness, balance, with expanding attentional demands and visual tracking.

We do not automatically learn to run. We fall down, we get up, and we try again. Children must be provided with the opportunity to develop their own personal sensory systems. Games teach the child in a subliminal way how to mature. Some "oldies but goodies are:"Blind Man's Buff," "Marco Polo," monkey bars, climbing equipment, tug-o-war games, etc.

These competencies evolve over time with repeated and varied experiences.

Emotional learning is paramount to all the other learning that we do and it is ongoing throughout life.

We must teach our children to be social. We exist in groups. Games that they can play against themselves to get their "personal best" as well as those they play with one or two others are excellent. Look for short-term games for the younger children. Remember that a four-year old has an attention span of about four minutes; so keep it novel and keep it short.

Some suggested toys that meet the above criteria are::

"Bop-It."

"Simon."

"Bumble Ball'

"Wiggly Giggly Ball"

"Rapper Snappers"

"Tactile dominoes"

"Koosh balls"

"Tactile balls"

"Whistle straws"

"Think and Go" Farm/City/ Etc.

Balance beams (you can make one out of 2" x 4" wooden strips from the hardware store)

Old appliance boxes that are lined with rug samples, etc. make great "hide-a-ways" and.

Zip lines

Rocking/sliding/turning toys; such as "Dizzy Disc."

Yarn blowpipes

Ring-toss

Jump rope

Jax

Board games—Chutes and Ladders

      Connect Four

      Checkers

      Battleship

      Scrabble Jr.

      Clue

Easels/paints

Tether ball

Rebounder

This is only a starter list, and should not be looked at as a complete mandate for acceptable toys.

Resources for Toy and Equipment Catalogs:

Troll: Learn and Play 1-800-247-6106

Manipulatives, make-believe.arts and crafts, some gross-motor.

Achievement Products for children 1-800-373-4699

Developmental toys, made for multiple children to use over time, good for therapy clinics.

Constructive Playthings 1-800-832-0572

Manipulative toys, problem-solving, etc.

Lakeshore Learning Materials 1-800-421-5354

Good resource for parents, teachers and therapists; wide range of toys and prices.

Play with a Purpose 1-800-451-4875

Focus on gross-motor development, interactive toys.

Pocket Full of Therapy 1-800-PFOT-124

Multiple gadgets and games for facilitating classroom activities.

Back for Basics Toys 1-800-356-5360

Good old-fashioned kid-powered toys.

Therapy Skill Builders 1-800-211-8378

Videos, and skill specific toys.

Sportime Abilitations 1-800-850-8602

Mainly gross-motor games and toys.

Sunburst 1-800-321-7511

Graded computer games that teach typing and other needed skills.

Oriental Trader 1-800-228-2269

Bulk toys for clinics, parties, etc.

Fun Express 1-908-290-0711

Same as Oriental Trader, but mainly bulk orders.

Pro-Ed 1-800-897-3202

Special education, rehabilitation, gifted children and developmental disabilities.

Kaplan; concepts for exceptional children 1-800-334-2014

Good source for large foam ramps, seating options, puzzles that are disability-inclusive.

S&S Opportunities 1-800-243-9232

Adapted play toys, mats, exercise equipment and inflatables.

Lily's Kids 1-800-545-5426

Wide variety of toys that can be used in multiple ways, gross to fine motor, puppet theatre, etc.

Professional Development Programs 1-800-651-8865

Sensory processing, postural control, skill development toys.

OT Ideas, Inc. 1-973-895-3622

Occupational therapy supplies for teaching fine motor skills.

Kinetic Kids 1-800-622-0638

Variety of toys and tools to teach sensory and life skills.

Cognitive Therapeutics Catalogue 1-800-444-9482

Interactive (anger, family relationships, academics, etc) board games for children 8-16.

Lekotek Toy Resource Helpline 1-800-366-PLAY

Hammacher Schlemmer 1-800-892-1063

And an "oldie but a goodie"—the ***Sears Christmas Wishbook***

For Development Programs for Schools, Organizations, Groups, etc. Also providing inservices for professionals with continuing education credits for occupational, physical, speech therapists and teachers.

Advanced Rehabilitation Services, Inc.

Chris Bosonoto Doane, President

413 Indian Hills Trail

Marietta, GA 30068

770-973-3466

IEP "Game Rules"

•Don't be afraid to be an advocate for your child.

• Do not be intimidated. Public schools generally have an overworked agenda. That is not your problem—it is theirs. What is expedient for them maybe very wrong for your child.

• Know the law(s), and make your requests within the law. They have to do what is written.

• Come into the meeting with your facts in order.

• If you invite specialists, make sure the school is informed ahead of time or the person will not be allowed into the meeting.

• You DO NOT have to sign anything at the meeting: get a second opinion, take time to think about it. If nothing happens of use or acceptability—you have the right to table the meeting.

• You have the right to object and/or ask for clarification.

• Don't be afraid of being labeled. a "troublesome parent." Be afraid of **not** being labeled it, sooner or later. The child needing your help had *best* have a meddlesome, adamant, inexorable parent. In fact, if you don't eventually find yourself.

• You have the right to request specific testing—(standardized, criterion_ref erenced and functional), and for it to be done within the designated time limits of the law of the State or County.

• You have the right to have it done again for validity—but read evaluations as a guide, not an indictment. It can help to keep goals realistic and minimize frustration for all.

• You have the right to have requests and responses documented—you do not

have to just take them at their word. You should get a copy of everything
written about your child.

• You have the right to ask why something is being recommended. You should
  also ask when and how and by whom

• Seek outside help if needed. Special education services are often put into
  the curriculum as related support services, this means that your child will
  only get help if they meet certain criteria. This is often for the very involved
  child: the average learning disability child is too "smart" for services, and too
  "problematic" for systems that teach to the "mean majority."

• Teach your child to stand their ground. If something doesn't sound right
  to them, they DO NOT HAVE TO accept it without checking with you,
  they can always call you to ask you if something sounds or feels right.

• But if the "team" writes it, they must do it—no alterations, changes,
  or modifications can be made by them without your prior knowledge
  and approval.

• You have the right to question specific grades.

• You have the right to a syllabus of each subject.

• You have the right to know what your child will be graded on and how
  each item will be weighted.

• You have the right to a conference at anytime.

• You have the right to limit the scope of the conference to a specific concern.

• You have the right to end a conference if it is not in keeping with the intent
  of the called-meeting.

• Do not keep the meeting going on forever—teachers are not being paid
  by the hour. But treat them as if you are the one paying. They have families

We are who we

are forever. Our

responses are what

we can change.

Teachers and Therapists

cannot cure a

learning disability.

and lives outside of school and their time should be respected. If more time is needed for resolution or closure ask for a continuation.

• You have the right to expect your concerns to be taken seriously and respectfully—and you should reciprocate this back to the faculty.

• You have the right to expect the school to teach to both your child's present performance level and to their assumed potential (by testing and observation)

• You should not "bulldozer" the meeting—make sure the right to speak and be heard is extended to both you and the faculty

• Come into the meetings prepared to compromise—but know your "bottom line"

• Do not allow a school official to be punitive—you can take your concerns to their supervisor.

• Your child should not be singled out because he/she is receiving accommodations.

• Your child should NEVER be threatened, be made fun of, or isolated because of modifications.

• Find an ally on the faculty—get advice from that person—"inside information" can be invaluable.

• Don't be afraid to be human. This is your child—they are hurting—and you are hurting for they. Your objective to get the kind of help that will ultimately get your child to the point of independence not just in school but in life. You are not out to change the system, just to use it in the best way possible for the benefit of all. For if the child succeeds, the school does too.

• Talk about feelings; school learning is about social as well as academic growth.

• Be motivated by true concern– not control. This is not about power, but empowerment for your child and the teacher.

• Reasonable progress commensurate with your child's innate abilities is the only real goal, but goals that are written on the IEP should be time specific and measurable

• Remember you are an expert too—who else at that table really loves your child--so make sure that you are a full participant of the "team", you don't have to "take it or leave it"

• If at all possible, present yourselves as a "team"—both parents, guardians, or significant others—when they see you "united" they will often get "behind" you more readily

• If you would call for apologies, then provide them if called for

• Say thank you

• Give praise not just complaints to the school officials and the teachers

• All of us "march to our own drum", make sure your child knows that his/her "music" is not wrong or odd, just unique and remind him/her that what is at one time "unique" often becomes the "standard" later—each star has its place in heavens—some just have to move around a bit to find just the right spot. Read *Leo the Late Bloomer* together often and talk about it.

Notes

"...A copy of the report

sent to private school

is requested under

the Freedom of Information

Act. No documents written

on behalf of my child,

as his legal guardian

can be withheld..."

If you have your child

in private school, you

are still entitled to

all of this information.

You can request testing

and services.

Transportation, location

(your child's private school

or his "home-based facility")

and timing will

need to be negotiated.

Never be afraid to ask.

Some Final Thoughts:

Do not "rescue" your child—give them the resources to be able to continually design and redesign themselves. For life is all about change; constant, inevitable, continual.

Life situations will be sometimes positive and sometimes negative. A successful person is able to learn and grow from both experiences.

Life's path will be both smooth and rough. The ability to be able to know how and when to right oneself is part of life's learning process, and it is only learned individually. It is essential for emotional health.

It is only from a feeling of well-being that permanent, positive learning occurs.

Questions to ask at an IEP

Outline the problem

What are the strengths and weaknesses, and how are they impacting the functional outcomes in the classroom?

Goal statements

Are they measurable goals? Will the student be able to accomplish the required tasks in a specific amount of time in an anticipated degree of accuracy?

Analysis of the problem

Have the team members generated & tested hypotheses related to the stated problems in an attempt to determine why the problem is occurring?

Intervention design

Given the hypotheses of why this is occurring, what strategies are going to be used, and do they follow a developmental sequence?

Evaluation and selection of interventions

What are the priorities?-Who will be implementing what?

Implementation

Selected interventions are monitored for effectiveness: who monitors what?

Evaluation of outcome

Final step: compare the student's current abilities with those at the onset of the intervention and measure what progress has and has not been made and state why. Also determine what needs to be done next. . .

End of year IEP Questions to ask

I. Original Status and how was that determined?

II. Initiating course work: *How* did it address initial strengths and weaknesses? *What* adaptive techniques were used that were different from traditional learning environments?

III. How was he after six weeks?—three months?—six months now?

IV. What were the specific weaknesses that were initially observed? (Not included in recent IEP.)

V. *How* were they and *when* were they resolved?

VI. What methods did you use? (Be specific.)

VII. What is the current status?

   a. **Academic:** (And how does this correspond to standardized State of Georgia requirements for each grade level?)

      1. Reading

      2. Math

      3. Language arts

      4. Science

   b. **Intellectual:**

      1. Performance

      2. Task behaviors

      3. Time concepts (Sequencing, getting work done "on time.")

      4. Task productions (Following directions, verbal written, demonstrated, repeated etc.)

      5. Task judgments (Independent, relies on teacher, friends, secure, insecure.)

      6. Retention (Long vs. short.)

      7. Organization

      8. Comprehension

         a) Auditory

         b) Reading

         c) Visual

         d) Directional

      9. Evaluation skills (How he accepts critical assessments, self-evaluations etc.)

c. Physical:

    1. Mobility (getting from one needed place to another (on time).

    2. Self-cares.

    3. Hand skills.

    4. Strength.

    5. Endurance.

d. Emotional:

    1. Response to authority figures.

    2. Frustration levels. (If there is a problem here please be specific, and list the primary and secondary concerns and how they are manifested during the the school day in academics, lunch room, art, music, physical education. etc.)

    3. Task response behaviors: avoidance, passive, fearful, requires (circle one):

    normal   somewhat more than average   excessive help from teacher–
How does he ask for it?

    4. Do they notice the needs of peers?

    5. Can they wait their turn?

    6. Are they easily distracted? Select one:
    noise   visual interference   both

    7. Sensitivities? How are they addressed in the classroom? When do they regularly appear? How fast are they resolved? When are they appropriate, When not?

VIII. How did you reach these determinations? What standardized and criterion-referenced standard observational forms/tests did you use, how did you select them and why?

XI. Plans? What — for what— how to be implemented?

IEP Suggestions for Parents
How to Have a Successful IEP Meeting

1.   *Have the right mind set.*

This meeting is your meeting. You and your child are the primary persons, not the teachers. You are the *expert* on your child.

"Uh-oh,

another thing for me

to deal with!"

2.   *Talk from the "heart."*

This is not about wanting to control the school or the committee. This is about your *fears* and your *dreams* for your child. This is about what your child *fears*, and what they *dreams*.

Go in with a prepared list. It is easy to get intimidated by the amount of "experts" around the table. Again—you are the expert on your child. Below   are samples of statements that may correspond to your situation:

If you could get

help with only

a few functional

concerns,

what would

they be?

Fears:

Some, any or all;

• The classes they are now in will limit their choices when they are older.

• The situation they are now in makes them feel like a loser.

• The peer group with whom they are placed is a negative influence.

I have noticed the following changes in their behavior. *(List them)*.

• They have all but given up. How can I help them want to learn?

• They are feeling rejected by both teachers *and* peers.

• I am afraid of these feelings of alienation.

• They seem depressed.

• Their eating habits have changed. *(Fear of eating-disorders)*

• Their potential is not being addressed.

• Their limitations are not being accommodated properly.

• They are "spinning their wheels." I do not see any learning or growth.

Dreams:

• I want them to have friends.

- I want them to feel like they belong at the school, like they have a niche.

- I want them to feel like someone cares.

- I want them to feel that despite his current level of functioning, someone has faith that they can make and reach their goals.

- I want them to feel they can exceed, succeed and thrive.

- I want them to feel connected to the learning process, the teachers and the school.

- I want them to feel that there is something special about theim that is positive and unique.

- I want them to feel liked.

- I want them to be able to make the right choices in peer situations.

- I want them to know how to discriminate between potentially positive and negative situations.

- I want them to feel that they can try something slightly beyond their reach.and that there are teachers here to help them meet that reach.

- And when this "growing up" is over, I want them to be an independent, content, goal-directed, successful adult.

3. *Now ask them how they can help you and your child reach these goals.*

4. *Set the IEP goals based on these dreams and fears.*

5. *Have the goals be specific.*

6. *The goals should be measurable.* (he will do _____by _____date-time_____.)

7. *A communciation system should be established for you to reach a key person if you have questions and/or concerns.*

8. *Everything should be in writing: accept nothing as an oral "promise."*

9. *Do not sign anything you are unsure of, you have the right to clarification.*

10. *You have the right to convene a meeting or adjourn one <u>for any reason</u>.*

11. *You have the right to bring other experts into the meeting, as long as the school is notified in advance.*

12. *For older children, they may want to be present. This often works against you, as the "team" then may feel they have to "talk tough" and it can inadvertently become a powerplay. Let them come in briefly, if they insist, either at the end or beginning of the meeting.*

N o t e s

Final Note:

These people are being *Paid*, they are not your friends, they are not permanent in your life, you do not have to please them. But be polite. Keep focused on your goals. Get them, if at all possible. on your "dream team". They are in the "successful kid business"; let them show you what they've got! Let them help you make your dreams, and those of your child, come true.

SECTION THREE
Guidelines
for Teachers

Developmental Markers for Pre-School Children

AGE	GROSS MOTOR	FINE MOTOR	SOCIAL
1 yr	•gets up fast/no help •walks unassisted •creepts upstairs •squats to play •hurls ball	•throws things on floor often •builds tower of 2 •holds two cubes in one hand •likes putting in/out •scribbles spontaneously •uses spoon in feeding • turns pages 2-3 at once • takes off shoes and socks	•5-10 word vocabulary •jargon •names a few pictures •understands simple verbal commands •2 word phrases •good movement of tongue, lips and palette.
2 yrs.	•walks- runs fairly well •up and down stairs 2 feet at a time •kicks large ball •picks up objects from floor •heel toe gait •toilet trained, dry at night if taken •walks on tip toes in play •jumps with both feet	•turns door knob • washes and dries hands • 6-7 tower of cubes • imitates cube train • puts on shoes, socks, pants • imitates vertical line and crude circle • over-hand grasp • snips with scissors • string beads • turns pages 1 by 1 • unscrews toy nut and bolt • recognizes primary colors	• refers to self by name • simple sentences and phrases • no jargon • begins to match 2 objects or pictures • plays meaningful with dolls andtoys • begins to use pronouns • begins to verbalize • immediate experiences • chooses meals

AGE	GROSS MOTOR	FINE MOTOR	SOCIAL
3yrs.	• walks upstairs alternating feet • walks downstairs both feet to 1 step • jumps from bottom step both feet • stands on one foot, moment of balance • rides tricycle using pedals • catches ball arms extended.	• holds pencil in hand instead of fist • removes shoes and pants • unbuttons, unlaces, unzips • feeds self with little spilling • 3 shapes in formboard • 10 block tower • copies crude circle • draws crude man on request • matches primary colors	• answers comprehensive questions • knows sex • uses plurals • identifies use of things in pictures • names 10 objects in picture and use • repearts 3 numbers • knows of accomplishments • attention span 2-4 minutes
4 yrs.	•throws ball overhand (dominance begins to be suggested). • stands on 1 foot for 2 seconds • tries to hop • jumps on toes	• independent eating • dresses and undresses • laces shoes • buttons • copies cross and cirle • washes hands and face	• follows 2-step direction • names primary colors • speaks in complete sentences • speech is understandable • less anxious to please
5 yrs.	• hops on one foot skips • alternates feet descending stairs marches • stands on each foot, with eyes open 5-10 seconds • stands on each foot with eys closed 10 seconds	• ties shoes • copies square • cuts on straight line • draws recognizable man • upon request tries to stay between lines when coloring • nests boxes correctly • copies triangle (6yrs.) • copies diamond (7 yrs.) • can walk backward heel toe	• follows 3-step request • correct use of parts of speech • counts 10 items • can group 4 out of 10 items • gives name age and address • 5 minute attention span • likes to please compiled by Susan N. Schriber Orloff, OTR/L Exec. Director, Special Children's Services

Some of the common
"glass half
empty" views . . .

Some Possible Teacher Reactions to a Special Needs Child:

• Forget about them.

• Phone home.

• Complain.

• Punish.

• Give them just the minimum because "they'll never get it anyway."

• Talk to the student find out how work is being done.

• Have the student keep a work log for 2-3 days.

• Help student brainstorm strategies for improved efficiency.

• Use a behavior checklist/Interest inventory to promote discovery

  of work/study styles.

• Suggest testing.

• Be supportive.

and some of the
"glass half full" . . .

Competencies Needed
for School Success

Neurological

Hearing

Balance– gravitational responses

Tactile

Visual

Cognitive (inclusive of attentional issues)

Emotional

Peer Interactions

Authority responses

Frustration levels

Task initiation/response patterns

Group skills

Physical

Mobility

Self-cares

Hand skills

Strength

Endurance

Intellectual

Performance Task Behaviors

    (rejection, motivation, curiosity, transitional skills, problem solving, etc.)

Time concepts (sequencing, getting work done " on time," etc.)

Task Production (following directions - verbal, written, demonstrated, repeated, etc.)

Retention (long vs. short term memory issues - ADD children.)

Task judgements (relies on teacher, peers, independent.)

Evaluation skills (accepting critical assessments, self evals.)

Age-Based Activities for School Success

School Competencies

Neurological: Hearing,

Balance • Gravitational Responses • Tactile

Visual • Cognitive (inclusive of attentional issues)

Suggested Activities:

Localization of various sounds in movement games...Treasure hunts...Under/Over tables chairs...Looking at mystery pictures while leaning over a table upside down.... Arranging a pattern while hanging upside down...Matching/sorting games...Finish the picture and/or patterns...Choose a cause or an effect of situation—i.e., if the glass stays on the edge of the table; and let them act out or draw the possible results...Utilize unfamiliar way, balance beams with 2 x 4's in various configurations.

Age 3	Age 4	Age 5
Keep it simple.	Add some independent decision making.	Require som guide independent decision making.
No more than 2-3 repetitive directions so that a pattern can be established and repeated.	Group instructions; 2 steps repeated, 2 more steps repeated, then go back and do one of #1.; for example	Make some directions non-repetitive; but sequential.
Walk them through the pattern at least two times, and then offer assistance as needed.	Keep tasks within specific time limits.	Include sorting tasks that require cross-referencing; i.e. items that are rough in texture and used in the kitchen, for example.
Expect some hesitations.	Do some things with eyes closed.	"Telephone" movement games that require them to remember and add to the list of things to do.
Expect some impulsive responses, expect some parallel play.	Change postures	
Provide clear structure.	Change the way a familiar object is used; such as a chair; a step stool, etc. Make tunnels, and "bridges" to cross over.	Recall movements with eyes closed.
Keep it short, Muliple short-term tasks are more readily responded to than one longer one.	"Buddy" the kids with partners.	Include all previous activities, upgraded.

Age Based Activities for School Success

School Competencies

Emotional: Peer Interactions,

Authority responses • Frustration levels

Task initiation/response patterns • Group skills

Suggested Activities:

Leadership activities...Role playing; use empathy: pretend you are old, blind...
Follow the leader, with alternate leaders...Games that require the use of their full
name and/or age...Memory recall games...Role playing...Integrating new words for

language enrichment...Time limitations and awareness...Ordinal awareness...
Dramatizations...Prepositional understandings with directions...Observational skills
...Personal space games, use hula hoops, etc.

Age 3	Age 4	Age 5
Attention span is 2-4 minutes.	Expect awareness of left and right with visual assists.	Attention span of five minutes or more.
Ask one-part questions, seek immediate answers.	Two parts that make a whole.	Shared activities.
Circles: have them find picture-specific items for each circle; i.e., concrete things found in a bathroom, den, etc. Have them work in groups, each person should have a specific task.	Choices, i.e., on a trip I want all of these things, about ten items; but you are going with friends and can only choose three, which three would you choose and why.	Sequential tasks that require waiting for the child's turn to come around again. *Trust* activities with parachutes, blankets, etc.
Classroom "monopoly" on the floor . Have them move about and "buy" and/or control certain blocks. Talk about feelings.	Junk box activities: what would you use for what; set up "in need" situations.	Unfamiliar tasks with no clear solutions, have the group decide how something should be done.
Sequential counting of objects, etc.	Take turns being blindfolded, walk around with a friend, let the friend describe something to you but not name it.	Verbal and motor "telephone" games. "Concentration" games. Make up a new language.

Age-Based Activities for School Success

School Competencies

Physical: Mobility,

Self-cares • Hand skills

Strength • Endurance

Suggested Activities:

Movement games that require postural changes...Cutting & pasting activities...Tracing...Sewing tasks...Pincer-grasp tasks such as those requiring the use of wooden clothes pins, key and combination pad locks, shuffling cards, hind-in-your hand games, pick up sticks, using a spinning top to make designs...Hanging upside-down off a chair and copying a design...Balance beams using 2x4s..."Fishing" for items using nets and magnets, for example...Body extremity isolation games; i.e.

Age 3	Age 4	Age 5
Keep it novel.	Use one roller skate to ambulate around a maze. Allow one foot for stability on the floor. Then expand task to use a buddy-on carpet: keep non-skate foot up to be "pulled" for a few inches.	Hanging games to incorporate kicking something or reaching out for something on an unstable surface
Short term.		
Fast paced.		Shoe tying.
Physically supported, i.e., use tricycles not bikes.		Lacing tasks that incorporate figure/ground discrimination.
Scooter boards that are about the length of their bodies for hand/arm strengthening.	Skate board activities.	
	"Pedal and Go" toys or moon shoes to change balance.	Role playing a time of day; i.e., morning, and teach a "pal" what to do -
Lacing tasks.		
Cutting "sunshines" and playdough, etc.	Catch beanbags or balls while standing on an inner tube.	Cutting out imbedded forms.
Wikki stick games.	Combat crawling and/or isolation of upper or lower body for movement.	Activities that require the crossing of the midline of the body; i.e., reaching across to get a needed supply, etc.
Strawberry pickers to pick up discrete items and place in a specific spot, etc.	Timed tasks/games.	

Age--Based Activities for School Success

School Competencies

Intellectual: Performance Task Behaviors (rejection, motivation, curiosity, transitional skills, problem solving, etc...Time concepts (sequencing, getting work done " on time," etc.)... Task production (following directions: verbal, written, demonstrated, repeated, etc.)... Retention (long vs. short term memory issues; ADD children)...Task judgments (relies on teacher, peers, independent)...Evaluation skills(accepting critical assessments, self evals).

Suggested Activities:

Sequential tasks that require students to make "on the spot" decisions—that may or may not affect the outcome of the task. Prioritizing tasks from given reasons: Give two directions one after the other, one to do now, one to do later, tell them that you cannot repeat them so they will have to listen carefully. Encourage "assists" such as picture-clues or assembled supplies. Establish criteria that they can "grade" themselves on.

Age 3	Age 4	Age 5
Have two task "pods," where all the necessary supplies for a particular task are out and available. Have them decide which pod they will go to first.	Increase the task "pods" to three.	Keep the "pods" at three but make them multiple steps (3 to 4).
Keep activities to one or two repetitive steps.	Two step repetitive tasks can be introduced.	Give a problem, such as you are a cave man and you need to build a hut but hammers are not invented yet: how can you build a hut? This can be a group project.
Discovery games for familiar items using familiar "clues."	Use transitions, i.e., from just finding a pasting to cutting-out and pasting, categorizing, etc.	
Treasure hunts.	Use a timer with a bell or a beeper and make them start and stop at specific times; if they did not finish have them think of ways they could have gotten the task done on time.	Have task carry over from one day to the next. Have daily completion goals.
Timed tasks that have "stop" and "go" indicators throughout the activity.		Utilize similarities and differences; matching and sorting tasks.
Tell a friend how to do something you were just taught.	Think up ways to use a familiar item in an unfamiliar way.	Use picture directions and sequential picture cards to tell stories.

How To Have A Successful IEP Meeting: IEP Suggestions For Teachers

1. Have The Right Mind Set.

This meeting is your chance to show offf your many teaching talents,

You are the teacher; emphasize creativity.

Your expertise is making familiar the unfamiliar to children.

2. You are obviously not doing this for the money, so talk from the heart.

This is not about wanting to control.

This is not about power.

You have joys, fears and dreams for the child. Talk about them.

What are your joys? And your frustrations?

What do you want from the child?

Go in with a prepared list.

3. You cannot help someone you do not like. So find something you like about him and focus on it. (Even if this child agitates you).

Samples of statements that may correspond to your situation. Some, any or all:

JOYS.

He always greets you when he comes in the classroom.

He has something interesting to say.

He is artistic.

You can tell his mind is always working.

He is sensitive to others.

He has a sense of fair play.

He follows the rules, and takes them seriously.

He has a sense of community about other members of the class.

He shares well.

He is creative.

His thought are often beyond his years.

His thinking is often "outside the box." This often confuses some more concrete children, which in turn complicates his social relationships.

FRUSTRATIONS.

He doesn't complete his work on time.

He sits fidgeting and wastes time.

He doesn't seem to know when or how to ask for help.

I can't figure him out.

He seems to sabotoge himself.

He is disorganized, and no matter how many times I help him get organized he cannot keep up with any system consistently.

He doesn't seem to understand the personal boundaries of the other children.

He says things that are inappropriate.

He tries too hard in social situations and this turns off other kids.

He has extreme reactions to corrective remarks.

He doesn't seem to take responsibility for his work, he always has some excuse or another.

I am afraid of hurting his feelings.

He seems to get hurt easily.

I feel he wants me to rescue him and I don't know how.

He doesn't stay on task.

I am looking for suggestions on how to channel his posirtive qualities into the classroom.

He is forgetful.

He demands a lot of my time.

He seems to need more stroking than other children.

•(It is probably true that you and the parents share the <u>same dreams</u>, and that you both are probably worn out!)

DREAMS

I want him to have friends.

I want him to feel like he belongs at the school, like he has a niche here.

I want hin to feel like someone cares.

I want him to feel that, despite his current level of functioning, someone has faith in him that he can make and reach his goals.

I want him to feel he can exceed, succeed and thrive.

I want him to be confident in himself.

I want him to feel connected to the learning process, the teachers and the school.

I want him to feel there is something special about him that is positive and unique.

I want him to feel liked.

I want him to be able to m ake the right choices in peer situations.

I want him to know when and how to ask for help.

I want him to know how to accept corrective remarks, and how to reject ones which are not valid.

I want him to know how to discriminate between potentially positive and negative situations.

I want him to feel that he can try something slightly beyond his reach and that there are teachers here to help him meet that reach.

And when this growing up is over I want him to be an independent, content, goal-directed, successful adult.

Now, as a team, think up ways the parents can help you and him rech these goals.

Set the IEP goals based on these dreams and fears.

Address the frustratin. let their resolutions be part of the goal plan.

Give the parents specific things to do.

A communication system should be established for you to reach the parent quickly if you have questions or concerns i.e. e-mail, a communication book, etc.

Everything should be in writing; and keep a file. Have all persons present at the meeting sign the minutes.

Do not push for an IEP signature if the parents are hesitant or nervous.

You have the right to suggest that the meeting be reconvened, tabled or adjourned if the tensions are to volatile—But first do everything to diffuse the negativity.

As for older children, understand they may want to be present. Even if you and the team do not want him in the whole meeting. let him come in briefly either at the end or the beginning. Remember: the child is the reason you are having this meeting.

Final note:

You are a teacher, not a genie. You are human. You have no magic wand. It is OK to say you need help. Benefit from the input of the parents. They are struggling too. Change takes effort. It can also be painful. You are aware of the ramifications of the struggles of children.

You are being PAID. The parents are not your friends, they are not permanent in your life. This is your career. This is you and your professionalism on display. Be polite, and keep foccused on the goals. Get the parents on your "Dream Team." You are in the Successful Kid Business......So show off what you've got!

Everyone wins, you look great, the parents feel you are with them and that they are not swimming upstream, and the message to the child is one of caring and concern.

SECTION FOUR
Occupational Therapy in Action

The following photos are examples of occupational therapy in action.

Promoting Kenistatic
Awareness
Using Jan Olsons's
"Handwriting
without Tears"
"Magic C"

*Figure-Ground
discrimination games*

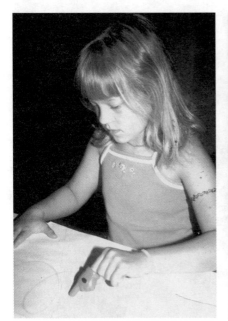

Visual Tracking

Part-whole perception

Design Copy
Using colored rubber bands

Plastic Easter-eggs help teach
"Crossing the mid-line"

Fun on the zip line to increase upper body strength and stability

Insecure balance

postual adjustment

Secure balance

postual adjustment

*Combining motor planning with
visual pursuit*

*Mobility / stability with
visual motor tasks*

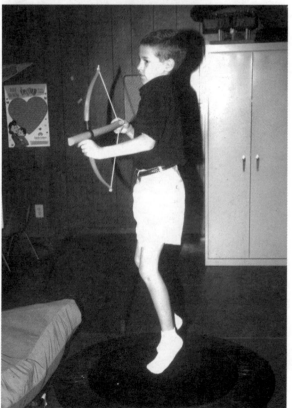

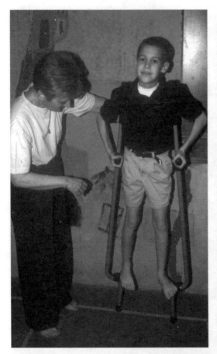

Weight shift and balance using pogo

stick & stilts

Movement throught a sensory tunnel

Perceiving body and space with vision occuded South paw tactile sock

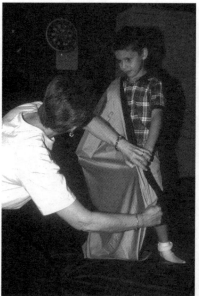
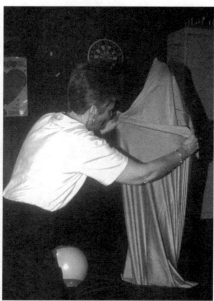

Learning to move and do at the same time

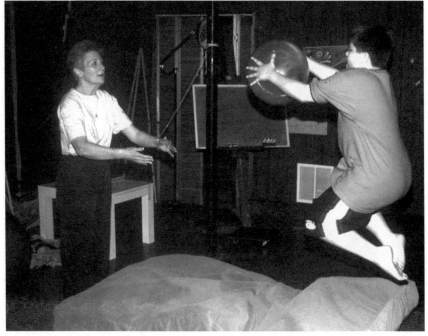

Using a flying turtle

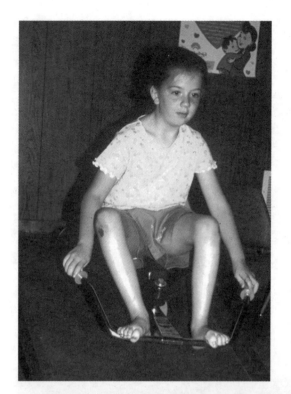

Crossing the mid-line.
Note: unstable
pattern here.

Balance beam tracking, weight shift with reaching and grasp and release activities

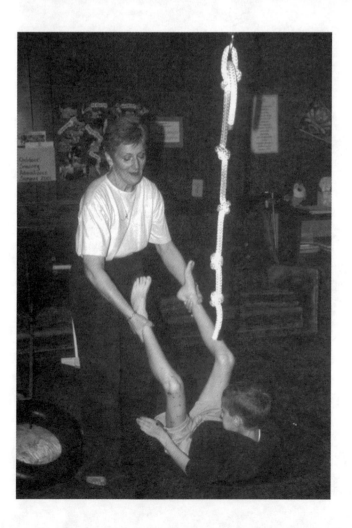

Falling from a zip line using alternative postures

Developing body and space security and awareness

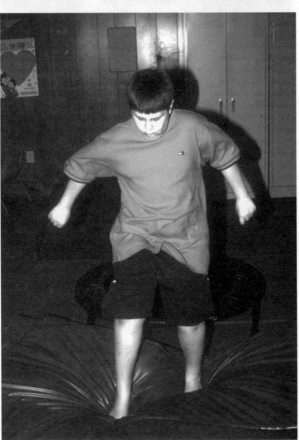

Using "southpaw" crash mat to increase motor planning and extension secure/insecure

Left fore arm rotation

Stable balance and co-contraction using handled skate board

Unstable balance and co-contraction using scooter board

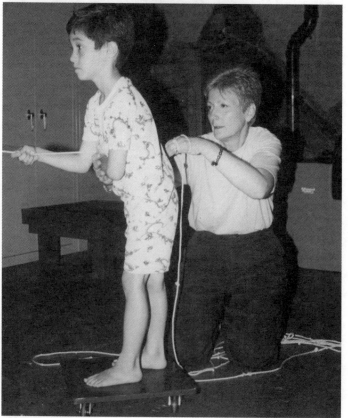

Postural adjustment

Combining motor planning with visual pursuit

Balance and tracking

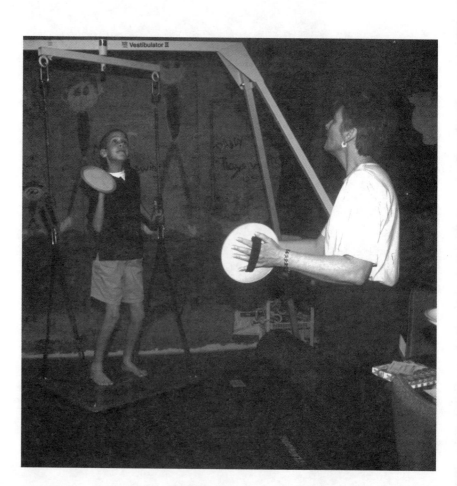

Using a pedal-and-go for weight shift, co-contraction, and mobility

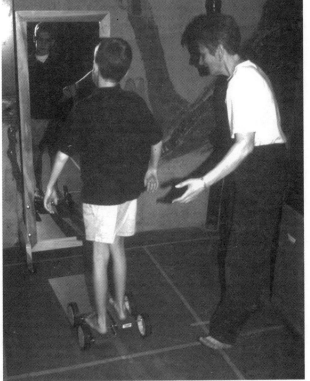

Mobility Stability with a visual target inclusive of receprical arm movements

SECTION FIVE
Student Writing Samples

writing samples

a. MF before
Therapy

My name is ᵢ _____ .
Make a funny story.

I felt _~~haukpey~~_ . I looked out
of my window. A _~~green~~_ cow was
coming along the street.

"Hello," said the _~~hilppy~~_ cow.
"I see you are _~~hungry~~_ . I like
people who are _green_ and have
~~hot~~ hair."

"Let's eat some _~~salitary~~_ food,"
I said. "Then we can play _nosie_
games together." We did.

"Where do you live?" I asked.
"In a _upside - down ~~house~~_ ." _~~said the~~_
cow. "I must go home now."

"Good-bye," I said. "Good-bye my
~~haukpey~~ friend."

Words that describe		
~~dark~~	~~hungry~~	~~noisy~~
silly	~~happy~~	~~upside-down~~
~~cold~~	~~purple~~	green
~~soft~~	salty	hot

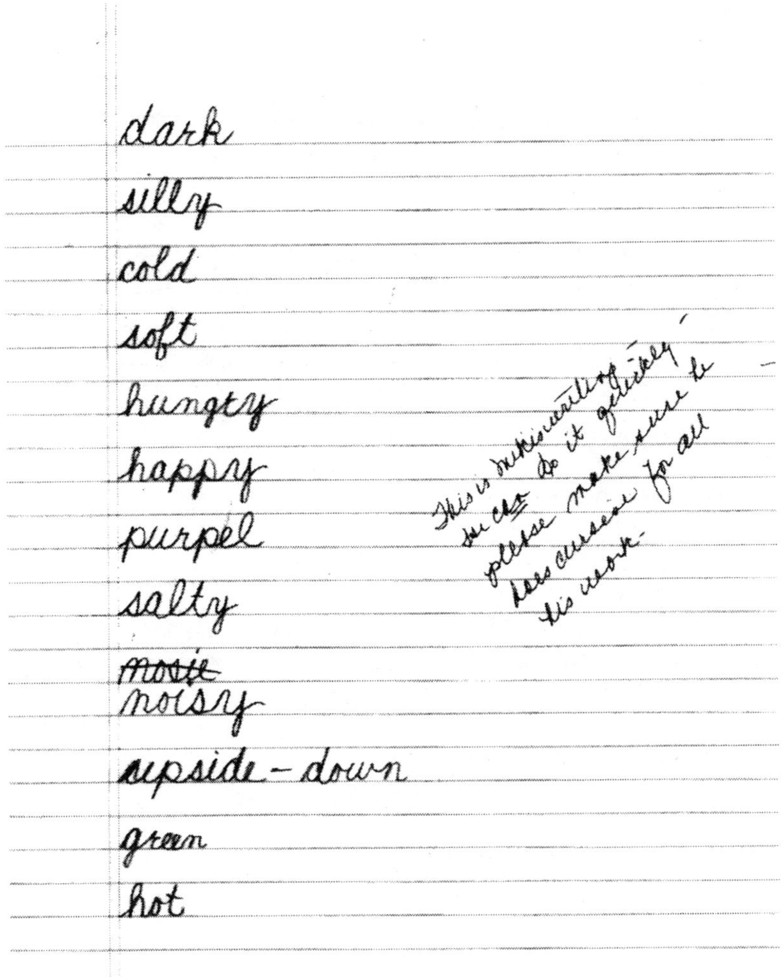

dark

silly

cold

soft

hungry

happy

purpel

salty

~~noise~~
noisy

upside – down

green

hot

This is mikiwritting to cho do it quickly please make sure he does arwea for all tis work

writing samples

a. M.S. Before
Therapy

Language Arts 7   Name
Mrs. Levine   Date

Letter to the Editor

Letters to the editor are written to express an opinion about a particular event or decision. Choose one of the stories from your anthology which deals with a controversial resolution, one upon which readers might have differing opinions. Write a letter to the editor, of at least four paragraphs in length, in which you express your opinion about how the conflict in one of your stories was resolved. Letters to the editor should be written in the first person (I). You should choose a resolution which you think was in some way unsatisfactory. Explain the conflict and resolution, and propose how the conflict might have been resolved more effectively. Fill in the worksheet below and use the notes to write your letter. You should include all of the information from your notes in the actual letter you will write.

Title and author: From Coffin To Rolls-Royce

List and describe the protagonists:
Sandy Thoms

Describe the setting:
World war II Athens

Explain the conflict and what led up to it: he was in a coffin and How he got out of it How does he get out to a nertert country

Explain how the conflict is resolved in the story:
He reaches the nartule cantrb and He rids in a Rolls-Royce

Explain why this resolution is unsatisfactory:
The car costs way to much to drive in after an escpe

Describe a new and original resolution and explain why it would improve the story.
A ride in a Van because it makes more sense because a Van costs less than a Rolls-Royce

4/10/98

A B C D E F G H I J K L M N O P Q R S T U V W X y

a b c d e f g h i j k l m n o p q r s t u v w x y z

abcdefghijklmnopqrstuvwxyz

a B C D

o B c O l c

1 2 3 4 5 6 7 8 9 10 11 12 13 14 15 16 17 18 19 20

The astronauts flew past the moon

the astronauts

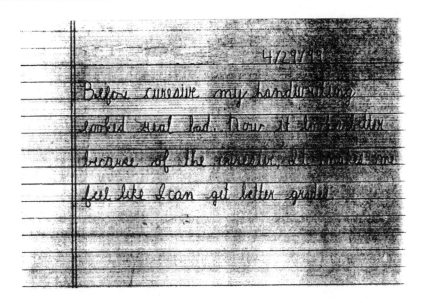

4/29/98

Before cursive my handwriting
looked real bad. Now it looks better
because of the cursive. It makes me
feel like I can get better grades.

writing samples

a. A. Before
Therapy

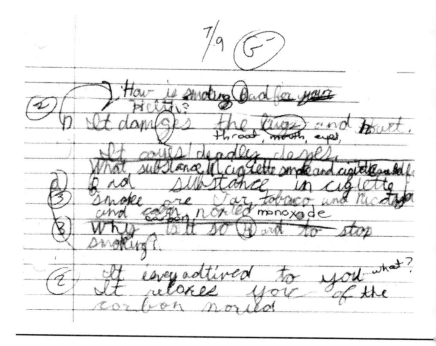

b. A. After
Therapy

1. How is smoking bad for your health?

It damages the lungs and heart

It causes deadly diseases.

What substance in cigaretts are bad for you?

The tar, tabacco, nicotine and carbon monoxide.

Why is it so hard to stop smoking?

It is very addictive to your body. It relaxes you because of the carbon monoxlde.

a. W. Before
   Therapy

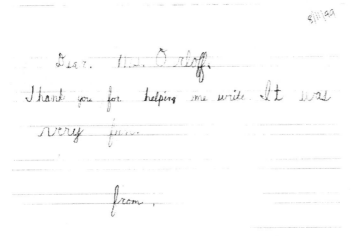

b. W After
   Therapy

writing samples

a. J. Before Therapy

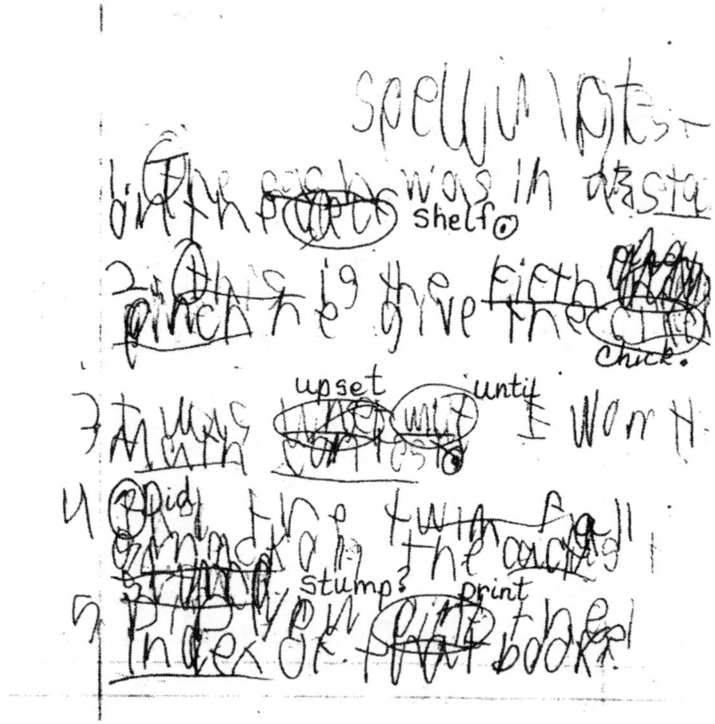

b. J. After Therapy

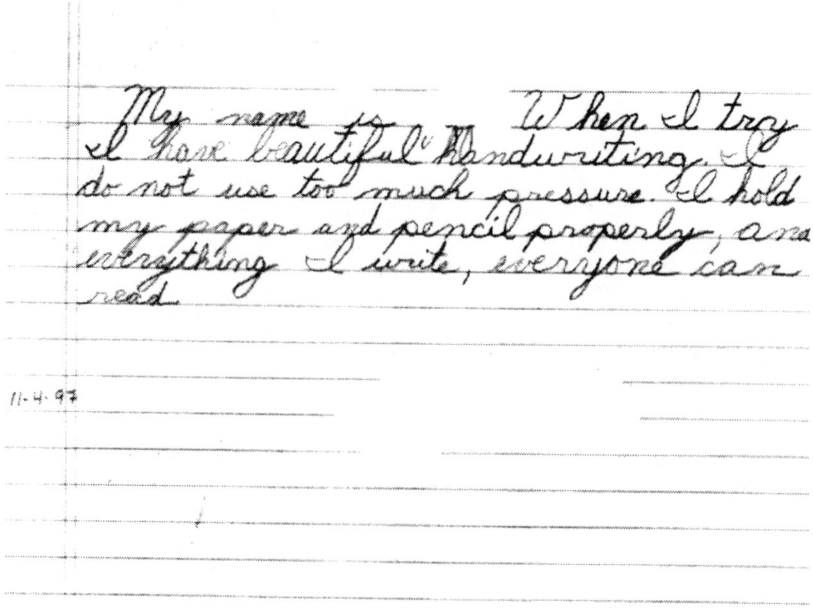

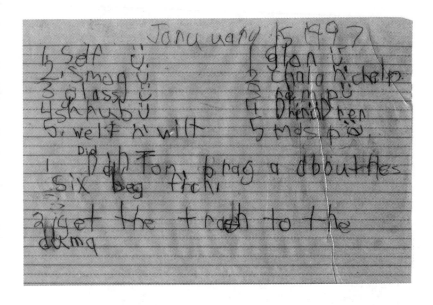

writing samples

a. B. Before Therapy

b. B. After Therapy

writing samples

a. T. Before
   Therapy

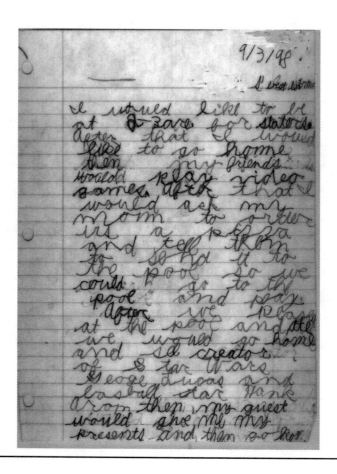

a. T. After
   Therapy

writing samples

a. L. After
   Therapy.
   (L destroyed all of her
   "befores", but was very
   proud of this.

lovely, lively and very luxurious.

SECTION SIX
Appendix and Resources

A FUNCTION-BASED GLOSSARY

Below is a glossary that has been developed to help parents and teachers understand common medical terms used to describe children seen by occupational therapists. Included for illustration, are ways in which a child may manifest these issues, a few examples of occupational therapy interventions, and how those treatment actives changes your child's related behaviors and performances.

Term Appearance OT Activities Changes

Apraxia—

a disorder of voluntary movement, consisting in partial or complete incapacity to execute purposeful movements, without impairment of muscular power or co-ordination. Children appear awkward or clumsy; more noticeable in large gross movements such as hopping and skipping. These kids seem to trip over nothing and bump into everything. Hitting a balloon up in the air, catching, kicking, and hitting balls in interactive games, problem solving while going through an obstacle course. Increased ability to break down activities into manageable parts and problem solve.

ADL—

activities of daily living: all tasks that are necessary for the maintenance of daily life, dressing, feeding, grooming, and initiating tasks. Children may reject tying shoes, or take off their shoes by kicking them off, leaving them tied, general appearance, and organization of personal items may seem "messy." Adaptive practice with the specific skills; organizing non-personal items in a game situation, figure-ground discrimination and in-hand manipulation games. Decreased rejection of self-care tasks and responsibilities; increased self-esteem, may develop a more relaxed response in social situations.

ADD-ADHD—

known as attention deficit disorder with the "H" standing for hyperactivity. It refers to the ability to focus on a task for the required time without unusual "drifting" out of the task arena; inclusive of organization of the required assignment. These are the kids that the teacher tells you needs to "try harder", is "lazy", "can do it when he/she wants to" is "manipulative", etc. In reality, this is a kid who is scared, disorganized, at time obsessive (in an effort to over compensate), and seems to have a hard time getting his homework started. Sensory-motor tasks that require different alert stages and "fidget" tasks that let the child cue into his/her own need to move and re-adjust. Intricate tasks that require both decision making and adaptive responses. Gross motor obstacle courses, posturally challenging games. Self-regulation of movement needs. Decreased moody responses; child seems more comfortable in his/her "own skin"; an understanding that they are ok, they can be in charge of themselves; that because they may not work as others does not mean "dumb".

Adaptation—

the ability to translate the needs of a task into a pattern that is more functionally accessible to the child; initially this is usually therapist facilitated, the goal being to have the child be able to do this for him/herself. This child tends to be very literal and does not seem to be able to re-direct his/her actions once in a task. They do not seem to "get it" that just repeating a way that is not working will eventually make it work. Discovering alternatives is hard. Working from familiar to unfamiliar and building on familiar schemes to create new skills in unfamiliar situations. These activities are presented in both the fine and gross motor formats as well as manipulative and cognitive based. Child learns to, become more independent and creative, as well as less fearful of unfamiliar situations. Often these kids are seen on the "fringes" of groups, and an increase in interactive responses is often noted.

Co-contraction:—

the ability of the muscles to hold a position; such as the "muscle-man" posture that little boys like to do. This child may seem lethargic and "floppy"; this situation is directly related to tone, which is that ability to hold a position against force. This is not strength. Resistance play utilizing scooter boards, "tug-o-war" games, zip lines, prone swing activities, climbing activities, obstacle paths, moving, pushing, pulling in game situations. Child exhibits increased ability to sustain him/herself in a task game situation. This is most noticeable in gross motor situations, but can also be seen in attention to directions and increased initiation of interactive activities with peers.

Cognitive—

Automatic—Learned habituated activities that can be done without a review of the process. Examples of this would be writing one's name, tying your shoes, etc.

Cortical cognitive functions, on the other hand, are slower, generally more labored and less fluid. An example of this might be using a map in town that you have never been to before, or putting a multi piece toy together, etc. Automatic:

This is an efficient way of doing "everyday" activities inclusive of but not limited the above mentioned ADL's.

Cortical—

Specifically the child with diagnosed and/or suspected learning issues looks like they are constantly "searching", there is a noticeable lack of fluidity of movement, with actions often appearing "jerky". It is not unusual to see sequencing problems with tasks as well. Automatic: generally is a matter of repetition until the "new" pattern becomes "old" and/or integrated. Teaching automatic functions greatly increases the child's independence.

Cortical—

when applied to unfamiliar situations a functional cortical style aids in problem-solving and enhances the child's ability to take a familiar scheme and apply it to an unfamiliar skill, thus expanding ability to make a variety of task adaptations. Increase in ability to enter into unfamiliar tasks, and significant decrease in fear of failure, and an increase in ability to follow and retain directions for both familiar and unfamiliar tasks. For some children who have learned behaviors when given new tasks—such as crying, etc.—a dramatic shift to more functional and assertive ways of confronting unfamiliar tasks that inherently has the risk of failure.

Flexion/extension Patterns—

The ability to come into and away from the body in both static (co-contracted/holding) or dynamic (movement/fluidity) modes. This child with poor lexion/extension patterns may have difficulty catching a ball because they stabilize their arms with their elbows close to the body; or their posture may appear "round shouldered", and sitting straight in a chair is a posture that cannot be sustained. In addition, these children often have difficulty with weight shift from one side of the body to the other as well as reaching across the midline of their bodies. They also tend to hold and write with the same hand. Stretching/pulling, activities on the tummy; such as scooter boards, extension in a net swing, standing on a moving bolster, weight shift activities on a tilt board, games while sitting on a one-legged stool, moving hands through a resistance (play dough, weighted box, etc.) and then using placement precision tasks that require stability on one side and movement on the other (usually dominant) side More relaxed performance styles in both the gross and fine motor realms. Less fidgety when sitting in a chair, increased ability to enter into interactive games with peers, increased self-esteem (they are not averting away from others, but rather meeting them "face to face." Increased postural stability; more fluid range of movements, increased willingness to try unfamiliar tasks; and when combined with a graded writing program, greatly improved handwriting!

Grasp—

the ability to hold a necessary object. This is most often used in reference to a style in which the child holds a pencil and/or utensils. Basically there are palmer (using the whole hand), static (over stabilized, rigid, intense) and dynamic (relaxed, movement oriented, fluid). There are many variations of grasp within these categories, but these are broad descriptions. This is often what teacher identifies as their students with poor handwriting, often accompanied by not being able to learn how to tie their shoes. They may not be astute enough to look at its precursors (flexion/extension, tone, etc), but they see a stressed grasp, slow production, sloppy work (often relegated as "not trying") and/or incomplete assignments. This is when the child is sent to the occupational therapist to "fix" the handwriting. Parents and teachers do not initially understand that this is a motor re-learning process that is not done in 2-3 sessions, but gradually over time (several months or more depending upon the severity). Pick up Stix, dominoes, lacing activities, using strawberry pickers or tweezers to put and place things; rubber band designs on a raised peg board, games with magnets of different sizes and strengths, sewing, various arts and crafts activities, stability/mobility patterns that facilitate holding on the non dominant side so that the dominant side can move. (Remember stability comes before mobility developmentally, so in order to write, which is movement, stability must be a secure posture). Confidence, pride in self and work, ownership of things that they do and make in school, they sign their name to their work so that anyone can see to whom it belongs, not just the teacher who has accommodated to deciphering a student's particular (non) style. Increased self-care abilities, improved grooming habits, less sloppy when they eat. More thoughtful execution of required tasks, increased competencies and independence with school and home assignments.

Kinesthesia—

the ability to have an internal body map that alerts and directs you through space. This is the ability for you to get from your car to you back door in the dark, or from your bed to the bathroom in the middle of the night without turning on a light; you "know" the path. These kids always seem to be bumping into things, they continually have a "lost" look about them; sending them to the office (in school) or to their room to get something often takes much longer than anticipated, and they are often accused of "dawdling". These kids "land" at a new destination almost every time they leave their stability point (i.e. class seat, "space" in front of the TV, etc.) and often they can appear somewhat ritualistic, having to always sit in the same spot in the car for example. Touch activities with a variety of textures, densities, shapes, and position of things. Blindfolded games, games in novel spaces, (odd shaped boxes, under tables, etc), doing a pattern first with vision and then without to stimulate internal memory of a particular pattern. Internal visualization games (with vision occluded), "imagine in your mind a circle, draw one as you walk on the floor, now remembering where your circle is, come over to the side of the room and place in your circle 3 things", for example, and this can be brought down to a desk top activity. More secure movement patterns, increase efficiency with tasks, faster response time when asked to do something, increased willingness to enter into unfamiliar situations, increased ability to enter into tasks where immediate success is not guaranteed. Increased agility, enhanced repertoire of "preferred" games, sports, etc. Less of a "loner," diminished "clinging" behaviors. In general, these kids become less tied to their immediate "world" gaining confidence in their internal environmental security.

Long term-short term memory—

Actually two separate functions, controlled by two separate areas of the brain. Short-term memory accounts for about 80% of our memory, and is the reason we can remember details for a test and then be unable to recall it an hour later. Long-term memory is a more complex process, actually holds less data than the short term centers but is considered "forever" which is why Alzheimer patients can speak of the past so clearly. Many children with learning issues have just the reverse of the average population. Their ability to keep data long term is superior, but in many cases, have significantly impaired short-term memory. Complicated by the fact that many of these kids are very bright, they look like they are being defiant, lazy, uninvolved, when the true issue is that they cannot remember instructions for new tasks, because they are stored in the short-term centers. Therefore, in order to learn something new they appear as if they are obsessively repeating something, when in fact they are memorizing the needed information. Strategies to learn more quickly are employed when "learning" the sequences to novel games and activities. Obstacle courses, and strategy games such as checkers, chess, connect four, can be non-threatening activities to develop alternative patterns that will be less cumbersome than the multiple repetitive techniques most commonly used. By taking a familiar game and "changing the rules," the child must adapt his/her thinking to participate. These types of tasks are often used simultaneously with other tasks working on other goals such as sequencing, and organization skills. Less last minute "rush hour" project completion. When a parent asks these kids on Tuesday "Do you have any homework"; they may answer "no" not, because they are avoiding responsibility, but because they honestly DO NOT REMEMBER until a peer asks them how the "project" is going. Parents and teachers see the panic phase and these kids get labeled "Johnny Come Lately's" when they are honestly lost. New strategies help them to avoid these pitfalls, but they must be learned in an orderly sequential program of graded activities. It is a rare child that can learn this on its own.

Motor planning —

is the co-ordination of the brain and the body to produce smooth, purposeful, successful movements. This child is your typical "klutz." They want to get to "B" but they do not know how to get off "A." These children are often labeled "passive aggressive" when they are not dawdling but truly "lost." Multiple gross and fine motor games to increase automatic repertoire of responses that will "fit," with minimum adaptation, into a new situation. Task problem solving and other (diminishing) supported tasks. Increased self-confidence, and the ability to participate in unfamiliar situations. Improved peer relationships, because now they can be counted upon in a group to do what they are assigned or have volunteered to do.

Muscle tone —

is the ability of a specific group of muscles to co-contract and stabilize for the purpose of a sustained movement. Writing at is a prime example of a task that requires both stability and mobility (to take notes, do a test, etc.) over time. These children appear to fatigue easily have primarily short-term endurance, and are not seen using recess to run around. These kids often pick a buddy to walk and chat with, and then feel rejected when that friend also wants to go off and run. Pencil grasp is either too intense (in an effort to compensate) or too fragile. Various activities inclusive of both gross and fine motor patterns. Stability comes from the center out, so securing trunk stability is the first step. This can be done in many ways; games in a resistance tunnel, scooter boards, tug-of-war skating, games that require the lifting and moving of weighted objects, in-hand manipulative skills. Improved manual dexterity. Increased ability to maintain an appropriate "alert" phase so that attention issues often diminish. Improved cutting and writing skills; increase speed in which familiar tasks are completed. Enhanced affectual responses.

Nystagmus—

is the reflex reaction of the eyes s to movement. Post rotation, there should be a noticeable excursion and duration of eye fluctuation. It is stimulated by the semi-circular canals of the inner ear, and literally let us know "what end is up". Children with a depressed or absent nystagmus, may superficially not exhibit any remarkable behaviors, but when parents are questioned, these are the kids that love amusement parks, and can do all the rides multiple times. This intense movement stimulates those "sleeping" reflex centers (vestibular system), and the movement, which could easily make us sick is soothing to them. Graded by intensity, duration, speed, and direction, movement activities on a variety of surfaces, that challenge their sense of gravity and promote an increased awareness of their bodies in space. These kids need supervision at play, because they can become "thrill seekers" in an effort to provide their system with the stimulation it is literally craving. Decreased restless behaviors, normalization of muscle tone, increased visual tracking, increased attention, increased ability to make postural changes as needed, increased stability/mobility patterns. Normalization of tactile (touch) responses, less distraction by extraneous stimuli.

Prone/supine—

refers to specific body positions. Prone is tummy down and supine is on the back. Stability/mobility patterns occur in both positions so it is important to develop both. They can exist exclusive of each other. These children have no overtly defining characteristics. Deficits in this area are discerned only upon specific testing. However, such deficits can impede success at sports, and may be contributor to random fatigue responses. Rejection of these positions can also be related to the touch system, so activities stress the synergistic relationship between movement and touch. Utilization of such activities include playing/pretend swimming in a "tactile box," twister-like games, etc. More agility and flow of movements. Less ritualistic behaviors (i.e. they don't always Have to have a special chair when watching TV, their bodies can now adapt to a variety of positions comfortably.

Proprioception—

is the muscle-bone joint internal awareness of the body and its specific parts that allows for postural security and position in space. It is important as a precursor to all purposeful movements. It is the proprioceptive feedback that allows us to make postural changes and adjustments as needed. These children are often described as the "Jell-O" kids, they look firm but they are really shaky. They cannot navigate from one place to another in smooth fluid movements, they have a lot of "stop and go" qualities to their habituated responses. They are constantly shifting from one position to another seeking out a comfort zone they cannot find because this system cannot locate where they are and what body part is needed to make the adjustments. Resistance activities with movement, Simon Says, Mother May I, balance beams and ramp activities; holding various dissimilar shapes and weights in each hand; moving through an obstacle course "wearing" novel objects of varying weights and degree of obstruction to movement. Activities that incorporate kinesthetic responses as well inclusive of sighted and occluded movement games. Increased control over one's own body, more secure movement patterns, and the ability to discern when a postural adjustment needs to be made and to what degree. Less random wavering of body in an attempt to maintain positional neutrality and stability.

SensoryModulation—

is ostensibly a reflexively self-regulated internal ability of the body to adjust to changes in sensory stimuli; like too much noise, walking on a rocking boat, having to pay cognitive attention to something while wearing a scratchy sweater, etc. Often these kids look out of control; they move in extremes; either every system in on or they are off; they have difficulty finding a middle ground and they are usually emotionally sensitive. They often require significant external support to maintain control. Multiple activities that incorporate the discrimination of 2 or more sensory stimuli in order to complete the required task. This could include combinations of sound and touch, or smell and visual discrimination. The ability to maintain a reasonable work pace with interference is the thrust of these tasks. Less frustration, fewer outbursts, less anger in task situations, increase control over emotions, increased tolerance of unfamiliar tasks, heightened awareness of internal mood shifts and the acquired ability to make appropriate changes in anticipation of the need.

Sensory Registration—

is the ability to receive and "catalogue" the incoming stimuli so that appropriate reactions and actions may take place. It is the degree to which we can be our own "biofeedback" machines so we can "feel" when the sensory input is appropriate or noxious. The children that have deficits in their sensory registration are known to over-react or under-react to specific stimuli. For example, this child may hit another kid while in the lunch line, perceiving a punch, when he only was slightly bumped. Another may not feel how hot a burner is in the chemistry lab, and so forth. Games that require the discrimination and classification of specific stimuli. Changing "What's my Line?" to "What's my sensory system?" allows the child in a risk free environment to experiment with various sensory situations and problem solve possible solutions. Less volatile, more personally responsible, increased comfort in unpredictable situations. Increased experimentation with trying out unfamiliar task scenarios. Increased anticipation of possible personal needs in a specific set of circumstances.

Stability/balance—

The laws of development are that before one can move they must first become stabile; and that means that one must have a secure starting point. For children, that is the rocking on all fours, the pre-walking weight bearing that gives them the foundation, the **balance** for movement. Stability is central—at the trunk of the body while balance total body and incorporates tone, flexion, extension, and motor planning proprioception and kinesthesia. Early walking toddlers are an example of movement before secure stability. They move with their legs farther apart, and arms stiff and outstretched; they are prepared to fall. Tightrope walker moves by holding a long balancing stick, these kids move using everything, they have to walk. They are usually stiff, fists clenched, and movement is jerky. As they grow they habituate stiff and move, instead of "flow and go" and they are constantly getting "stuck". This often becomes demonstrated in school by poor handwriting. They try to hold the paper and write with one hand, and are usually supporting their body with the other. Activities that require both stability and mobility for successful completion; such as laying prone on a platform swing and stopping yourself with your non-dominant hand and stacking cones or picking up a puzzle piece with the other; roller skating games, scooter activities, skateboarding, balance beam games, etc. Games that require the kids to start from still, move, and perform a specific motor task and then resume and repeat the pattern. These kids may be good soccer players because they are always on the move, but cannot play basketball or baseball as well. Less sedentary, more amenable to participation in group games, improved handwriting increased organizational abilities, less easily frustrated. In other words, this is a child who is now in the "drivers seat" where before, the "car" (i.e. body) was driving him/her, and they were stiff, holding on "for dear life"; to compensate for insecure stability and balance mechanisms.

Strength/endurance—

Strength is the actual amount of force the body is able to exert in order to lift, move, or place something. Endurance is the length of time this activity can be sustained. Children with good strength but poor endurance work in bursts with significant "down times." In this case, other sensory motor factors are influencing the child's ability to stay on task. Strength can occur without endurance but it is endurance rarely exists without strength. Weight bearing games, wheelbarrow walking with specific placement tasks required, scooter board games, timed activities (a personal "beat the clock"), multi-tasking several (2 or more) activities that require weight shifting, gross motor, and fine motor alteration. Increased participation, assignments done with less "procrastination" (which was really their need to re-group, because they literally ran out of "steam").

Symmetrical/non—

This is when both sides of the body are moving together; synchronized. An example of this would be both arms flexed at the same time. Asymmetrical or non-symmetrical movements are what we normally do automatically. We walk swinging our arms back and forth, children skip, we hold on to the counter when we have to get something almost out of our reach, and we may be totally weight bearing on just when side when we do this. These are the "bullet" kids. They move as a single unit with little or no reciprocal patterns, usually in very stiff postures, in either a "full speed ahead" or "full stop" mode. Sometimes this is much more subtle. The child can look like there is nothing wrong, and then little "stuff" gets snagged, like handwriting, math papers, precise agility in sports (these kids can play well, but they are usually in the offensive positions.). Vestibular swing activities, using the platform to be prone to push and fixate while completing another task; weight shift games on the bolster swing, getting to move the bolster in a circle by just shifting your body; wearing in-line skates pull yourself hand over hand along a designated path; standing one foot on another, one arm on table for stability, and paint, do a puzzle, make a "Lite Brite' pattern; jump every other foot on a trampoline, etc. Less rigidity of movements, more willing to try unfamiliar tasks, a reduction in fear of falling, increased scanning abilities, normalization of body tone, increased ability to focus on task presented instead of trying to do a specific task and at the same time be focused on holding yourself steady.

Tone: hypo/hyper—

Not to be confused with strength which is power; tone is co-contraction over time to hold a functional position. One's endurance is directly related to one's tone. Hypo tone, or low tone is loose, wiggley, and unstable. Hyper tone is extreme, tense and over stabilized. Children with hypo tone seem to "poop out" quickly, writing is usually very light, and related skills such as coloring and cutting reflect this instability, looking "wispy" in nature. Hyper tone kids look like robots, stiff, unbending, clenched hands. Fine motor skills are also affected do to the fact that most of their energy goes to keeping themselves steady. These kids handwriting is very pressured and jerky, and they will tell you "writing makes their hand hurt." Whole body approach, for it just not the hands that need to normalize tone, although it is there that it becomes the most obvious. Multiple weight bearing activities, hanging from zip lines, pulling back on a large "Nerf" shooter, skating a pushing a heavy basket from place to place. For the hands, cutting resistive surfaces such as play dough and cardboard, using strawberry pickers to pluck small beads from a dough or Styrofoam ball, finger symbols, etc. When tone is brought into functional ranges, total body movement becomes more fluid. Low tone kids are noted to play more in gross motor activities; high tone kids are noted to be able to relax more, go to sleep easier and frustrate less "automatically." Fine motor skills inclusive of but not limited to handwriting markedly improves, as do most dressing, grooming, and other self care skills.

Transitional activities—

these are the tasks that help us go from on situation to another. It's like an automatic "pre-1st" for our bodies; we are not quite ready for a big move so we take a little one instead. Children that find it hard to transition from one task to another often fixate on the task at hand, sometimes obsessively. They resist any changes in their lives and react strongly to externally imposed changes. In toddlers this can be observed with the child that will reject all toys but one (type, i.e. dinosaurs for example), will not greet any unfamiliar people even with parental support, and seldom initiates interactive play unless in a totally familiar environment. Structured sessions with choices, with noted beginnings and endings to all discrete tasks. Increasing their "comfort zone" of change by slowly, decreasing the amount of "advance warning" when a project is about to end and another begin. Stopping a task midway through to go onto something else and then coming back to it later. This can be incorporated with many activities; building a cardboard box house, paper mache', puzzle creations, etc. A decrease in situational anxiety, increased ability to think through tasks, and to reduce them into component parts; to be able to self select points at which the task may be stopped and resumed later; increased acceptance and interest in a variety of toys, less fearful of new situations and people; increased problem solving skills.

Vestibular stimulation—

technically this is the fluid movement in the semi-circular canals of the ear, that trigger eye movement, touch perception, balance, midline, gravitational, and vibratory responses in each of us. It is our "putting it all together" system. It takes all of the above mentioned sensations and movements and communicates to them to create the movement desired. It is our "this end is up" alert system. Children with vestibular problems usually fall into two major categories: too little or too much. The kids with too little are your roller coaster forever kids, they never seem to get dizzy, and they are always on the move because the stimulation is comforting for them. Like adults feel when their ears are stopped up, their whole bodies feel dampened down. For kids with too much, any movement makes them sick and they are your sitters, they want to be still. For the low kids the more spinning, moving, up-ending activities the better. For the high kids a slow program of graded movement activities that will expand their tolerance and acceptance of movement is recommended. Use skate boards, scooters, scooter boards, games on ramps, obstacle courses that require positional shifts, etc. Increase in accuracy of all tasks that require the utilization of both sides of the body; reading (both eyes), walking (both feet), eating dressing, playing, as well as increasing the ability to tolerate, anticipate, and eventually welcome novel movement experiences. Decreased exaggerated tonal responses increased fine motor skills inclusive of handwriting.

Vision/perception—

Vision is only visual acuity; how far and near can you see with and without correction (i.e. glasses). Perception is translating that acuity into meaningful symbols, organizing them and re-organizing them for problem solving, task attack skills, and discrimination. There are seven realm of perception: basic discrimination, visual memory, visual sequential memory, and visual closure, figure-ground, visual form constancy, visual closure (part-whole perception).

These are often your "homework war" kids. Every piece of work looks like hieroglyphics to them and so they habituate a fight/flight reflex and come up with a thousand reasons not to get to the task. This is often interpreted as avoidance; sometimes these kids are labeled passive-aggressive when all they really are is scared. Children may have some, but rarely do have all these systems impaired. Standardized testing is the only way to discern which systems are strength, and which are a weakness. By capitalizing on the stronger ones, and helping the child feel successful the therapist can help transform these deficits into positive tools for increased function. Some activities will be paper and pencil, but many will be gross motor manipulative as well. Decreased fear, more compliant with assigned chores, increased organization, decreased rejection of "have to" work, increased social security, they have learned to transform a miss-perception into something meaningful and functional and as they feel more secure in the world they become more socially at ease. Increased problem solving, and ability to use familiar, known skills to help complete those that are unfamiliar.

What does Uncle Sam Say About all of This?

Quotes from the IDEA, Americans w / Disabilities Act (Public Law 101-336) and the Educational Act (Public Law 94-142).

IDEA

This law incorporates the learning situation with defined transition services as.....

"...a coordinated set of activities for a student, designed within an outcome oriented

process. which promotes movement from school to post-school activities including post-secondary education, vocational training, integrated employment, including supported employment, continuing adult education, adult services, independent living or community participation. The coordinated set of activities shall be based upon the individual student's needs, taking into account the student's preferences and interests and shall include instruction, community experiences, employment development, and other post-school adult living objectives, and when appropriate acquisition of daily living skills and functional vocational evaluation." —(20 U.S.C. § 1401 [a][19])

And said, true to form and function, in Uncle Sam's own anti-nimitable style. The effect however has been eloquently spelllike. A sea change, total and ubiquitous, oversweeping the barrier landscape of outer obstacles and inner exclusion. The latter though, what with its tougher prejudices, is the hurdle that meets the movement of these, Our Kids, out in the world. Wheelchairs and crutches gain sympathies that brains do not. The Americans w/ Disabilities Act took some care then to deal expressly with the interior bordertowns along the terrain of the ouside world. And seeks still to smooth gradiently down both our streetside curbs and the edges of the ungainly flipped-about letters of the quietly dyslexic. Soon, it will be as safe to show one openly as the other. And the way will be as clear.

The ADA demonstrated a major ideological shift in the perception of Disability. The commitment has changed from "fixing & curing" to "accomodating and modifying."

SECTION 504
REHABILITATION ACT of 1973

Common Questions & Answers

1. What is 504?

2. Who is responsible for the enforcement and investigation of compliance with Section 504?

3. Who is eligible for 504?

4. Who determines if a student is eligible for 504?

5. How does the Student Support Team determine if a student is 504 eligible?

6. What is a Section 504 Accomodation Plan?

7. What are the parent's rights under Section 504?

8. What are reasonable accomodations?

9. What are some examples of classroom and facility accomodations?

10. What are the guideliness for special teat accomodations under Section 504?

1. What is 504?

Section 504 of the Rehabilitation Act of 1973/ Public Law 93-112 is a comprehensive law which addresses the rights of handicapped ("disabled") persons and applies to all agencies receiving federal financial assistance. Eliminating barriers to education programs and services, increasing building accessibility, and establishing equitable employment practices are thoroughly and specifically addressed in Section 504 regulations. The section states, "…No otherwise qualified handicapped individual shall, solely by reason of his/her handicap, be excluded from the participation in, be denied the benefits of, or be subject to discrimination under any program or activity receiving federal financial assistance." The regualtion makes it clear that the failure to provide a "free appropriate public education" to a disabled student covered by Section 504 is discrimination which violates the Act

2. Who is responsible for the enforcement and investigation of compliance with Section 504?

The Office for Civil Rights (OCR). Federal financial assistance to a local school district is contingent on compliance with this and all other civil rights laws. The OCR may determine that federal funds should be withheld from local school systems which are not in compliance with civil rights legislation.

3. Who is eligible for 504?

In 1973, when the Rehabilitation Act was passed, 'handicap' was the acceptable term for a mental or physical impairment. Today, "disability" is preferred and promoted. But either refers to a person who (1) has either one which substantially limits one or more major life activities, or (2) has a record of such an impairment or (3) is regarded as having such an impairment. To qualify for protection under either law the individual must have a physical/mental disability that substantially limits a major life activity such as caring for oneself, performing manual tasks, walking, seeing, hearing, speaking, breathing, LEARNING, and working. Examples include Tourettes Syndrome, epilepsy, sickle-cell anemia, asthma, serious illness or injury.

ADD/ADHD.

When a school is informed that a student has Attention Deficit Disorder, the school is required to make appropriate accommodations in educating the student. These strategies can be documented on the SST Strategies/Minutes Form. For example, if behavior is the manifestation of the condition, then the successful development of a behavior management plan meets the school's obligations under federal law.

If the student is manifesting attention problems which are affecting learning, the Student Support Team can develop strategies to address those within the regular classroom using the SST. Where the ADD results in behavior or attention problems so severe that they cannot be regularly accommodated the school is Section 504-obligated to provide special services to enable the student to benefit from an educational program. Students may qualify under IDEA as a student suffering from an 'other health impairment.' The

Student Support Team should then determine if they need to make a referral to special education for consideration of OHI eligibility

4. Who determines if a student is eligible for 504?

Referrals begin at the local school level and are made to the Student Support Team. The SST process should be followed:

Initiate services.

Clarify disability and needs.

Generate a 504 Accommodation Plan.

Evaluate plan.

Monitor.

Reevaluate.

5. How does the Student Support Team determine if a student is 504 eligible?

To qualify for protection under Section 504, the individual must have a physical or mental impairment that substantially limits a major life activity such as caring for oneself, performing manual tasks, walking, seeing, hearing, speaking, breathing, learning and working. Three questions to consider in determining whether a person's impairment substantially limits one or more major life activities: (1) What is the nature and severity of the impairment? (2) How long will it last or is expected to last? (3) What is its permanent or long term impact or expected impact? Temporary, non-chronic impairments that do not last for a long time and that have little or no long term impact usually are not considered to be "disabilities".

6. What is a Section 504 accommodation plan?

Although a written plan is not required in federal regulations, it is advised and practically, it makes good sense that the plan be in writing. Parents should be notified and parental rights given. (see attached sheet)

7. Where are parents rights under Section 504?

(see attached sheet)

No. 10: This is our major conern!

8. What are reasonable accommodations?

Extended time for test/projects/assignments, and all items listed on the psychological. Reasonable accommodation in the school setting is a modification or adjustment of educational programs to afford students with disabilities equal opportunity to access the programs. Schools must provide reasonable accommodations to students with disabilities unless and schools can show that the requested accommodations would impose undue hardship. The concept of undue hardship includes any action that is unduly costly, extensive, substantial, disruptive, or would fundamentally alter the nature of operation of the program.

9. What are some examples of classroom and facility accommodations?

Refer to attached sheets for accommodations in the areas of communication, organization management, alternative teaching strategies, and student precautions.

10. What are the guidelines for special test accommodation under Section 504?

An accommodation plan must be on file for each student for which modifications will be made. The plan should outline instructional modifications appropriate for the student during regular classroom instruction. Testing modifications consistent with other instructional modifications should also be outlines in the plan. It is not appropriate to make testing modifications unless the appropriate documentation is on file. Students who are tested under Section 504 guidelines and receive modification on the ITBS may be coded 99. Modifications made on a norm-referenced test will invalidate the results.

SECTION 504
STUDENT ACCOMODATION PLAN

I.   Name: _____ VII DOB: ___/___/___

II. School:_____Grade: _____

III. Date of Meeting: _____

IV: Describe the disabling condition: _____

_____

_____

_____

_____

V.   Describe how the disability affects a major life activity: _____

_____

Educational Impact: _____

_____

VII. Describe the reasonable accommodations that are necessary: _____

_____

_____

_____

_____

VIII Location of Accommodations: ( ) Regular Class   ( ) Other

IX. Review/Reassessment Date: _____

X.   Participants name: Title: Date:

_____   _____   _____

_____   _____   _____

_____   _____   _____

XI. I have participated in the development of this plan and have received a copy of the

Notice of Section 504 Rights.

Parent Signature: _____ Date: _____

Classroom and Facility Accommodations

As local districts develop policies and procedures for guiding the referral and identification of students determined to be handicapped under Section 504, it is critical that information concerning this law and its impact on local school districts be shared with principals and building-level staff. The intent of Section 504 is to accommodate for differences within the regular education environment. For this to be accomplished, all staff must be provided with awareness activities and given specific information concerning the district's procedures for dealing with Section 504 referrals.

As individual students are identified, the classroom teacher may need specific training in the area of the identified handicap (e.g., training from the school nurse on danger signs of an impending asthma attach, training from a physical therapist on correct positioning of a wheelchair-bound student at his/her desk, etc.) The following classroom facility accommodations are presented as examples of ways in which Section 504 handicaps may be successfully addressed within the regular education environment.

I. Communication:

    A. There may be a need to modify parent/student/teacher communications.

      for example:

- develop a daily/weekly journal
- develop parent/student/school contacts
- schedule periodic parent/teacher meetings.

    B. There may be a need to modify staff communications.

- identify resource staff for extended time testing as needed
- network with other staff
- schedule building team meetings
- maintain on-going communication with building principal

    C. There may be a need to modify school/community agency communication.

      For example, with parent consent:

- identity and communicate with appropriate agency personal working with student.
- assist in agency referrals
- provide appropriate carry over in the school environment.

II: Organization/Management

    A. There may be a need to modify the instructional day. for example:

- allow student more time to pass in hallways
- modify class schedule.

B. There may be a need to modify the classroom organization/structure. For example:

- adjust placement of student within classroom (e.g., study carrel, proximity to teacher, etc.)
- increase/decrease opportunity for movement
- determine appropriate classroom assignment (e.g., open versus structured)
- reduce external stimuli

C. There may be a need to modify the district's policies/procedures. For example:

- allow increase in number of excused absences for health reasons
- adjust transportation/parking arrangements
- approve early dismissal for service agency appointments

III. Alternative Teaching Strategies

A. There may be need to modify teaching methods, for example:

- adjust testing procedures (e.g., length of time, administer orally, tape record answers)
- utilize materials that address the student's learning style (e.g., visual, tactile, auditory, etc.)
- adjust reading level of materials.

IV. Student Precautions:

A. There may be a need to modify the classroom/building climate for health purposes. For example:

- use an air purifier in classroom
- control temperature
- accommodate specific allergic reactions

B. There may be a need to modify classroom/building to accommodate equipment needs. For example:

- plan for evaluation for wheelchair-bound students
- schedule classes in accessible areas.

C. There may be a need to modify building health/safety procedures, for example:

- administer medication
- apply universal precautions
- accommodate special diets

SECTION 504
PARENT RIGHTS

1. Right to file a grievance with the school district over an alleged violation of Section 504 regulations.

2. Right to have an evaluation that draws on information from a variety of sources.

3. Right to have program/services decisions made by a group of persons who know the needs of the student, the meaning of evaluation data and programs/service options.

4. Right to be informed of any proposed actions related to eligibility and plan for services.

5. Right to examine all relevant records.

6. Right to receive all information in the parent's/guardian's native language and primary mode of communication.

7. If the student is eligible under Section 504, the right to periodic reevaluations and an evaluation before any significant change in program/service modifications.

8. Right to an impartial hearing if there is a disagreement with the School District's proposed action.

9. Right to be represented by counsel in the impartial hearing process.

10. Right to appeal the impartial hearing officer's decision.

Now—

Go out and

follow your own

best advice!

Susan Orloff, OTR/L.

Notes

N o t e s

N o t e s